VCE Units 3 & 4
BUSINESS MANAGEMENT

DEBRA McNAUGHTON

2023–2027 STUDY DESIGN

+ course summary notes
+ exam practice revision questions
+ detailed, annotated solutions
+ study and exam preparation advice

STUDY
NOTES

A+ VCE Business Management Study Notes
4th Edition
Debra McNaughton
ISBN 9780170465137

Publisher: Caroline Williams
Project editor: Tanya Smith
Editor: Leanne Peters
Series text design: Nikita Bansal
Series cover design: Nikita Bansal
Series designer: Cengage Creative Studio
Production controller: Karen Young
Typeset by: Nikki M Group Pty Ltd

Any URLs contained in this publication were checked for currency during the production process. Note, however, that the publisher cannot vouch for the ongoing currency of URLs.

Acknowledgements

Selected VCE examination questions and extracts from the VCE Study Designs are copyright Victorian Curriculum and Assessment Authority (VCAA), reproduced by permission. VCE ® is a registered trademark of the VCAA. The VCAA does not endorse this product and makes no warranties regarding the correctness or accuracy of this study resource. To the extent permitted by law, the VCAA excludes all liability for any loss or damage suffered or incurred as a result of accessing, using or relying on the content. Current VCE Study Designs, past VCE exams and related content can be accessed directly at www.vcaa.vic.edu.au.

For product information and technology assistance,
in Australia call **1300 790 853**;
in New Zealand call **0800 449 725**

For permission to use material from this text or product, please email **aust.permissions@cengage.com**

ISBN 978 0 17 046513 7

Cengage Learning Australia
Level 7, 80 Dorcas Street
South Melbourne, Victoria Australia 3205

Cengage Learning New Zealand
Unit 4B Rosedale Office Park
331 Rosedale Road, Albany, North Shore 0632, NZ

For learning solutions, visit **cengage.com.au**

Printed in China by 1010 Printing International Limited.
2 3 4 5 6 7 26 25 24

CONTENTS

HOW TO USE THIS BOOK. vi
A+ DIGITAL FLASHCARDS. vii
PREPARING FOR THE END-OF-YEAR EXAM. viii
UNITS 1 TO 4 OVERVIEW. xii
FOR STUDENTS xii
FOR TEACHERS xii
ABOUT THE AUTHOR xii

UNIT 3

MANAGING A BUSINESS

Chapter 1 Area of Study 1: Business foundations

Area of Study summary		2
Area of Study 1 Outcome 1		2
1.1	Business foundations overview	3
	1.1.1 Business types	3
	1.1.2 Business sizes	4
1.2	Business objectives	5
	1.2.1 To make a profit	5
	1.2.2 To increase market share	5
	1.2.3 To improve efficiency	6
	1.2.4 To improve effectiveness	6
	1.2.5 To fulfil a market need	6
	1.2.6 To fulfil a social need	6
	1.2.7 To meet shareholder expectations	6
1.3	Stakeholders	6
	1.3.1 Stakeholder types and their interests	6
	1.3.2 Conflict between stakeholders	8
1.4	Management styles and skills	8
	1.4.1 Management styles	8
	1.4.2 Management skills	10
	1.4.3 Relationship between styles and skills	12
1.5	Corporate culture	12
	1.5.1 Corporate culture – official and real	12
	1.5.2 Importance of corporate culture	13
	1.5.3 Indicators of corporate culture	13
Glossary		14
Revision summary		16
Exam practice		18

Chapter 2 Area of Study 2: Human resource management

Area of Study summary		21
Area of Study 2 Outcome 2		21
2.1	Human resource management (HRM)	22
	2.1.1 HRM overview	22
	2.1.2 HRM and business objectives	22

2.2   Motivation   22
    2.2.1   Motivation overview   22
    2.2.2   Maslow's Hierarchy of Needs   23
    2.2.3   Locke and Latham's Goal Setting Theory   24
    2.2.4   Lawrence and Nohria's Four Drive Theory   25
    2.2.5   Comparison of motivation theories   26
    2.2.6   Advantages and disadvantages and effects of motivation 26
2.3   Training   28
    2.3.1   Training overview   28
    2.3.2   On-the-job versus off-the-job training   28
2.4   Performance management   29
    2.4.1   Performance management strategies overview   29
    2.4.2   Management by objectives   29
    2.4.3   Appraisals   29
    2.4.4   Self-evaluation   30
    2.4.5   Employee observation   30
2.5   Termination   30
    2.5.1   Termination overview   30
    2.5.2   Types of termination   31
    2.5.3   Entitlement considerations   31
    2.5.4   Transition considerations   31
2.6   Workplace relations   32
    2.6.1   Workplace relations overview   32
    2.6.2   Participants in the workplace   32
    2.6.3   Awards and agreements   34
    2.6.4   Dispute resolution process   34
Glossary   36
Revision summary   38
Exam practice   40

Chapter 3 Area of Study 3: Operations management

Area of Study summary   44
Area of Study 3 Outcome 3   44
3.1   Operations management overview   45
    3.1.1   Operations management and business objectives   45
    3.1.2   Key elements of operations of manufacturers and service providers 45
    3.1.3   Corporate social responsibility and operations   46
3.2   Operations management strategies   47
    3.2.1   Technological developments   47
    3.2.2   Materials management   50
    3.2.3   Quality management   51
    3.2.4   Waste minimisation   52
    3.2.5   Lean management   53
3.3   Global considerations   54
    3.3.1   Global sourcing of inputs   54
    3.3.2   Overseas manufacture   54
    3.3.3   Global outsourcing   54

Glossary	55
Revision summary	57
Exam practice	59

UNIT 4

TRANSFORMING A BUSINESS

Chapter 4 Area of Study 1: Reviewing performance – the need for change

Area of Study summary		65
Area of Study 1 Outcome 1		65
4.1	Business change	66
	4.1.1 Proactive and reactive approaches to change	66
	4.1.2 Key performance indicators to analyse performance	66
4.2	Change management theories	68
	4.2.1 Lewin's Force Field Analysis theory	68
	4.2.2 Driving and restraining forces	69
	4.2.3 Porter's Generic Strategies theory	70
Glossary		72
Revision summary		73
Exam practice		74

Chapter 5 Area of Study 2: Implementing change

Area of Study summary		79
Area of Study 2 Outcome 2		79
5.1	Leading change	80
	5.1.1 Leadership in change management	80
	5.1.2 Management strategies to respond to KPIs	80
	5.1.3 Management strategies to seek new business opportunities	81
	5.1.4 Management strategies to develop corporate culture	81
5.2	Change management theories	82
	5.2.1 Senge's Learning Organisation theory	82
	5.2.2 Lewin's Three-step Change Model	84
	5.2.3 Low- and high-risk strategies to overcome employee resistance to change	85
5.3	Considerations after implementing change	86
	5.3.1 Effect of change on stakeholders	86
	5.3.2 Corporate social responsibility considerations	87
	5.3.3 Review to determine effectiveness of change	87
Glossary		88
Revision summary		89
Exam practice		91

SOLUTIONS. 96

9780170465137

HOW TO USE THIS BOOK

The *A+ Business Management* resources are designed to be used year-round to prepare you for your VCE Business Management exam. *A+ Business Management Study Notes* includes topic summaries of all key knowledge in the VCE Business Management Study Design 2023–2027 that you will be assessed on during your exam. Each chapter of this book addresses one Area of Study from the Study Design. This section gives you a brief overview of each chapter and the features included in this resource.

Area of Study summaries

A+ Business Management Study Notes includes topic summaries of the key knowledge in the VCE Business Management Study Design 2023–2027 which is assessed in the final exam.

Concept maps

The concept map at the beginning of each chapter provides a visual summary of the key knowledge of each Area of Study outcome.

Key knowledge summaries

Key knowledge summaries in each chapter sequentially address all key knowledge of the Study Design.

Revision summary

Use the revision summary at the end of each chapter to complete comprehensive notes of all key knowledge points.

Exam practice

Exam practice questions are at the end of each chapter to test you on what you have just reviewed in the chapter. These are written in the same style as the questions in the actual VCE Business Management exam. There are some official past exam questions in each chapter.

Short-answer questions

There are approximately 20 short-answer questions in each chapter, often broken into parts. These questions require you to apply your knowledge across multiple concepts. Mark allocations have been provided for each question.

Solutions

Solutions to practice questions are supplied at the back of the book. They have been written to reflect a high-scoring response and include explanations of what makes an effective answer.

Explanations

The solutions section includes explanations of what is required to write a high-scoring response and identifies where a number of possible options would be considered to be correct.

Icons

The icons below occur in the summaries and exam practice sections of each chapter.

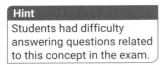

Hint
Students had difficulty answering questions related to this concept in the exam.

Hint and note boxes appear throughout the key knowledge summaries to provide additional tips and support for certain key knowledge.

©VCAA 2015 SB Q3

This icon appears next to official past VCAA questions.

One of these icons appears next to all questions to indicate whether the question is easy, medium or hard.

About *A+ VCE Business Management Practice Exams*

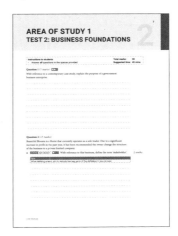

A+ VCE Business Management Practice Exams Units 3 & 4 can be used independently, or alongside the accompanying resource *A+ VCE Business Management Study Notes*. *A+ VCE Business Management Practice Exams* features 14 topic tests comprising original VCAA-style questions, official VCAA questions and two pull-out practice exams. Each topic test includes multiple-choice and short-answer questions, and focuses on one key knowledge area of the VCAA VCE Business Management Study Design 2023–2027. There are two complete Unit 3 & 4 practice exams following the tests. Like the *A+ VCE Business Management Study Notes*, detailed solutions are included at the end of the book, demonstrating and explaining how to craft high-scoring exam responses.

A+ DIGITAL FLASHCARDS

Revise key terms and concepts online with the A+ Flashcards. Each topic glossary in this book has a corresponding deck of digital flashcards you can use to test your understanding and recall. Just scan the QR code or type the URL into your browser to access them. Note: You will need to create a free Nelson MindTap account.

https://get.ga/aplus-vce-busmgmt-u34

PREPARING FOR THE END-OF-YEAR EXAM

Here are some ideas to assist you in your preparation for the Business Management exam:

The exam is months away

There is still a lot of time, but there's no point in wasting it. Start to prepare for your exam now in little ways:

- Use class time effectively. Ask questions, take notes that are meaningful.
- Complete all homework tasks.
- Set up an effective study area at home. Do you work better with or without music? Are there too many distractions in your study area?
- Try to do actual activities rather than just reading your notes, as these will reinforce concepts.
- Focus on trying to improve in the areas that emerged as problems in your assessment tasks. Perhaps you don't know your definitions well enough, or maybe you don't read the questions properly.
- Start preparing concept maps as topics are completed. These concept maps can be reminders of the key points in topic areas while they are still fresh in your mind. They can then be used later on, as the exam draws nearer.
- Use the revision questions at the end of each chapter of this book to help you to revise key areas.

Revision strategies leading up to the exam

- Revise the main points again by re-reading all of the chapters in this book. You may have forgotten many of the concepts from Unit 3 at this stage of the year.
- Try to answer the revision questions again to see how much you have remembered.

The exam is next week

November already? Where did the year go? Your feelings about this will probably depend on how well prepared you are. It's never too late, however, to improve your chances of doing well in the Business Management exam. Try these strategies:

- Read through your study notes, making your own concept maps (or adding to those prepared earlier in the year) of key terms and the way they link together.
- Put these concept maps all over the house – in your bedroom, on the fridge, next to the bathroom mirror – wherever you might see them and be reminded of the information.
- Write a set of true/false questions (and answers) for each of the five Areas of Study, then try to answer one set each night leading up to the exam.

The exam is today!

You had a proper night's sleep and you have used your time effectively leading up to today. Try to make the experience as positive as possible:

- Make sure that you eat well (minimise junk food) to keep your energy levels up throughout the exam.
- Try not to study the whole course on the day of your exam. Perhaps go over a few areas that are of concern and remind yourself of examiners' comments about common mistakes made by students in the exam in recent examination reports that relate to the current Study Design.
- Allow plenty of time to travel to school or your examination venue.
- Give yourself some quiet time to compose yourself before your exam begins.
- Use the exam writing time wisely. Use the number of marks and the number of lines as a guide for how much to write.

In the exam

Start to plan your responses in reading time (without picking up a pen obviously). This can be crucial in making the most of writing time. Perhaps write some brief notes when writing time starts.

Mark the command words so that you know how to address the question. You may have a system for doing this that you learned in class.

Where to start? That's up to you. Some students start with a question that they can easily answer to give them a positive start. Others start with Section B so that the case study material is still fresh in their minds after reading time.

Timing is important. Don't write everything you know for every answer. Answer the question as it is written, otherwise you may run out of time and risk not completing the exam.

Section B instructions state: *Use the case study provided to answer the questions in this section. Answers must apply to the case study.* Keep this in mind even if the question does not specifically mention any aspect of the case study.

Command words

It is impossible to achieve full marks for answers if you have no idea what the question is actually asking you to do. It is very important that you take note of the command words before you start to answer the question. The following list should assist you in understanding the core command words. Please note, however, that the list is not VCAA endorsed. The VCAA has released a comprehensive glossary of all command words, which can be found on their website.

Analyse	Break the concept down into its essential elements to clarify what it is really about.
Compare	Explain what is similar and what is different.
Define	Provide the meaning of the term without using the same words – wherever possible also give a supporting example to be safe.
Describe	Talk about the features of the term with a bit of detail.
Discuss	Write a lengthier response, where you cover more than one point of view (i.e. pros and cons, strengths and weaknesses, benefits and costs).
Evaluate	Carefully look at the different arguments (for example, for and against) and discuss the value of each. Finally, form an assessment of which argument is more valid (has more weight). It's a bit like a discuss question taken one step further.
Explain	Talk about the concept in detail (how, who, what, where and why).
Identify	Simply list the words required of you (used very seldom on its own in exams because it is too simple and does not test depth of understanding; often combined with something else, e.g. 'identify and describe ...').
Justify	Defend your opinion and back up what you've said. Why did you select or write that particular answer?
Outline	A very brief overview of what the term is about.
Propose	Suggest something that is appropriate or suitable.

Concept groups

Students must also be familiar with the names of groups of concepts so that you can instantly recognise what the question requires. This list may assist. Perhaps add others as you study the course:

Types of businesses	Sole traders, partnerships, private and public companies, social enterprises and government business enterprises (GBEs).
Management styles	Autocratic, persuasive, consultative, participative and laissez-faire.
Management skills	Communication, delegation, planning, leadership, decision-making and interpersonal.
Key performance indicators (KPIs)	Percentage of market share, net profit, rate of productivity growth, number of sales, rates of staff absenteeism, level of staff turnover, level of wastage, number of customer complaints, number of workplace accidents.
Key elements of operations	Inputs, processes and outputs.
Human resource management strategies/practices	You should refer to things the human resource manager could do to improve a situation. These will most likely come from the methods to manage employees, such as training or implementing performance appraisals, motivation strategies or workplace relations.

Strategy groups

There are 11 Key Knowledge points in the Study Design that refer to strategies. Revising them this way may assist you to sort them out clearly before you sit the exam. Don't forget that these are the minimum that you must know. There could be specific questions on any of these.

Key Knowledge	Strategy examples
Unit 3 Outcome 1 – Business foundations	
	No strategies in this Area of Study
Unit 3 Outcome 2 – Human resource management	
Motivation strategies including:	• performance related pay • career advancement • investment in training • support strategies • sanction strategies
Performance management strategies to achieve both business and employee objectives, including:	• management by objectives • appraisals • self-evaluation • employee observation

Key Knowledge	Strategy examples
Unit 3 Outcome 3 – Operations management	
Strategies to improve both the efficiency and effectiveness of operations related to technological developments, including:	• the use of automated production lines • robotics • computer-aided design • computer-aided manufacturing techniques • artificial intelligence • online services
Strategies to improve both the efficiency and effectiveness of operations related to materials, including:	• forecasting • master production schedule • materials requirement planning • Just In Time
Strategies to improve both the efficiency and effectiveness of operations related to quality, including:	• quality control • quality assurance • Total Quality Management
Strategies to improve the efficiency and effectiveness of operations through waste minimisation in the production process, including:	• reduce • reuse • recycle
Strategies to improve the efficiency and effectiveness of operations related to lean management, including:	• pull • one-piece flow • takt • zero defects
Unit 4 Outcome 1 – Reviewing performance – the need for change	
	No strategies in this Area of Study
Unit 4 Outcome 2 – Implementing change	
management strategies to respond to key performance indicators and/or seek new business opportunities, including:	• staff training • staff motivation • change in management styles or management skills • increased investment in technology • improving quality in production • cost cutting • initiating lean production techniques • redeployment of resources (natural, labour and capital) • innovation • global sourcing of inputs • overseas manufacture • global outsourcing
Corporate culture and strategies for its development	The Study Design does not specify which strategies must be studied. It is plural, so more than one is required. Use your notes and student book to assist you with writing a few strategies for each of these.
low-risk strategies to overcome employee resistance, including:	• communication • empowerment • support • incentives
high-risk strategies to overcome employee resistance, including:	• manipulation • threat

UNITS 1 TO 4 OVERVIEW

The Business Management Study Design was written to follow the stages that many businesses follow from the initial idea, through to the stages where it is established and is looking to change to make improvements.

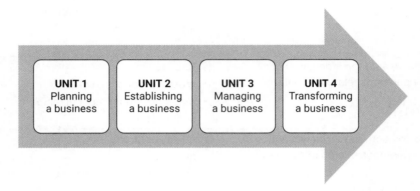

While studying Units 1 and 2 provides students with a more complete picture of the life cycle of businesses, it is not essential. Units 3 and 4 are complete and stand alone in terms of the knowledge covered. That is, there are no concepts that are required from Units 1 and 2 that are not in Units 3 and 4.

FOR STUDENTS

There are a number of ways that *A+ VCE Business Management Study Notes* could be used by students. As a supplement to a textbook, *A+ VCE Business Management Study Notes* can clarify points that were not clear. Students can then return to their textbooks for more detail and further examples. As a revision tool, this book should prove to be extremely useful. It can be used to revise topic areas throughout the year after they have been studied in class, or prior to assessment tasks. *A+ VCE Business Management Study Notes* contains clear outlines of topic areas, and the questions and answers can assist in identifying areas that require further revision leading up to the exam.

FOR TEACHERS

A+ VCE Business Management Study Notes contains suggestions for real business examples and website details that may be useful. This is essential as the VCE Business Management Study Design that began in 2017 and was revised in 2022 states that examples should be no more than four years old. For beginning teachers, it can provide an easy-to-read overview of concepts with which they may not be totally familiar.

Readers are advised to check the VCAA website for any changes that may be made to the Business Management Study Design, the Advice for Teachers and details regarding the examination.

ABOUT THE AUTHOR

Debra McNaughton

Debra McNaughton is an experienced teacher of Business Management and Economics and is currently the Deputy Principal at Sacred Heart College, Kyneton. She is the author of all previous editions of *Business Notes* and was co-author of early editions of *A+ Business Management Practice Exams*. She gained experience working in both the private and public sectors before moving into education. Debra has contributed to the Victorian Commercial Teachers' Association through its journal, *Compak*, and in the provision of Professional Learning for teachers at the VCTA's annual conference, *Comview*, over many years. She has also held many roles with the VCAA including State Reviewer and Assistant Chief Assessor for Business Management in recent years.

UNIT 3
MANAGING A BUSINESS

Chapter 1
Area of Study 1: Business foundations 2

Chapter 2
Area of Study 2: Human resource management 21

Chapter 3
Area of Study 3: Operations management 44

Chapter 1
Area of Study 1: Business foundations

Area of Study summary

This is the area of study that provides you with the building blocks you will require for the other areas of study in Units 3 and 4. It has the key concepts and terms that you need to understand so that you can use them properly and in context when required.

It includes the different types of businesses, their objectives and stakeholders. It looks at the skills that managers need and the styles of management that they may use. It also introduces the concept of corporate culture.

In addition to the knowledge that is required, you need to be able to apply the concepts to contemporary case studies from the past 4 years. These can be Australian examples or global businesses.

Area of Study 1 Outcome 1

On completing this outcome you should be able to:

- analyse the key characteristics of businesses, their stakeholders, **management styles** and skills, and **corporate culture**.

The key skills demonstrated in this outcome are:

- identify, define, describe and apply business management concepts and terms
- interpret, discuss, compare and evaluate business information and ideas
- analyse case studies and contemporary examples of business management
- apply business management knowledge to practical and/or simulated business situations.

VCE Business Management Study Design 2023–2027 p. 17, © VCAA 2022

1.1   Business foundations overview

1.1.1 Business types

In order to understand the different types of businesses, we need to look at the ownership arrangements. The VCE Business Management Study Design lists the following:

- sole trader
- partnership
- private limited company
- public listed company
- social enterprise
- government business enterprise.

Sole trader

Sole traders are individuals who own their own business.

Benefits of operating as a sole trader

- The owner has full control of all business decisions.
- Owners do not have to set up a business tax file number. They may use their individual tax file number to lodge tax returns.
- The owner gets to keep all profits (after taxes have been paid).

Difficulties of operating as a sole trader

- The owner has unlimited liability. This means that their personal assets as well as business assets can be seized if debts are not paid.
- It can be difficult for the owner to take time off work, which would mean leaving the responsibility of running the business with another person.

Partnerships

Partnerships are businesses that are owned by 2 to 20 people. Examples include law firms, doctors' practices and retail businesses. Sometimes family members form partnerships, while others are formed because of common business interests.

Benefits of operating as a partnership

- They are not expensive to set up.
- Each partner may contribute funds to assist with setting up the business.
- Each partner will bring different skills, experience and abilities.
- Partners can share the workload, making it more manageable.
- More ideas can be put forward, as each partner contributes.

Difficulties of operating as a partnership

- Each partner has unlimited liability. This means that their personal assets as well as business assets can be seized if debts are not paid.
- There may be difficulties if the partners disagree on the direction that the business should take.
- There are more legal requirements such as lodging a partnership tax return with the Australian Taxation Office (ATO) each year.

Companies

Companies are legal entities that are separate from their **owners** (the companies' **shareholders**). There are two main types of companies in Australia: public and private.

Public companies are those with more than 50 non-employee shareholders and are usually listed on the Australian Securities Exchange (ASX). They raise funds by offering securities (commonly referred to as shares) for sale to the general public. The number of shareholders can be unlimited. They must have the word 'Limited' or 'Ltd' at the end of their company names if they are limited public companies. Examples include Woolworths Group Limited and Qantas Airways.

Private companies are those that have no more than 50 non-employee shareholders. They can raise money from shareholders and **employees** of the company and, in some cases, from the general public. Private companies must have the words 'Proprietary Limited' or 'Pty Ltd' in their names if they are limited proprietary companies. Examples include Linfox Pty Ltd and Blundstone Australia Pty Ltd.

Strengths of operating as a company

Companies have limited liability compared with other structures. This means that the shareholders' own assets cannot be seized if the business is in debt.

Difficulties of operating as a company

There are many more complex legal requirements, such as registering with the Australian Securities and Investments Commission (ASIC) and complying with the *Corporations Act 2001* (Cwlth). Another difficulty is that the shareholders may have diverse priorities which can be difficult to satisfy.

Social enterprises

Social enterprises buy and sell goods or services as standard businesses do, but their main objective is to fund or support social causes such as reducing poverty, providing employment for various societal groups or tackling environmental problems (see the section on **business objectives** later in this chapter). They do not rely on donations as charities do. The strengths and difficulties vary according to the ownership type. Social enterprises are usually either companies limited by guarantee (a form of company that is regulated by ASIC) or non-trading cooperatives where the members do not keep the profits, but put them back into the enterprise to support the social causes. One of the best-known examples is Thankyou.

Government business enterprises

Government business enterprises (GBEs) are organisations that are owned by a level of government, but they have been corporatised. That means that they run as businesses and are expected to make a profit. An example at state level is VicRoads, which generates its income from issuing driving licences, vehicle registrations and so on. A federal example is Australia Post. The general public cannot buy shares in these organisations unless the government decides to privatise them (sell them to the non-government sector).

> **Hint**
> Find examples of all the different types of businesses that are described in this chapter. Start by asking class members for examples with which they are familiar. These may be their parents' businesses or workplaces, or the students' employers at their part-time jobs.

1.1.2 Business sizes

While this is not a key knowledge point, it can be helpful to understand what is meant when reading about businesses. Sometimes the strategies that a **manager** decides to put in place will be different depending on the size of the business. For example, a training program for a total of five employees might be quite different from one for 500 employees.

The Australian Bureau of Statistics (ABS) states that the number of people employed determines the size of the business (see Table 1.1).

Number of employees	Business ownership options
No employees	These can be sole proprietorships or partnerships without employees.
Fewer than five employees	These are known as microbusinesses and include the non-employing businesses (see above).
More than 5 but fewer than 20 employees	These are usually called small businesses. They normally have independent ownership. The owners provide most of the operating capital (funds) and make the business decisions.
More than 20 but fewer than 200 employees	These are medium businesses. They can be independent sole traders or may be private or public companies.
More than 200 employees	These are large businesses. Usually, but not always, these will be private or public companies.

TABLE 1.1 Business size based on the number of employees

Source: Australian Bureau of Statistics. (2002) Small Business in Australia.
ABS cat. no. 1321.0. ABS, Canberra. www.abs.gov.au/ausstats/abs@.nsf/mf/1321.0

Note: The ABS does not classify agricultural businesses according to size.

1.2 Business objectives

It is common for medium to large businesses to have a mission, vision and/or value statement. These statements can provide the direction and boundaries in which the organisation should operate. They are usually created by senior management, although there may have been staff input, and all other decisions made and the objectives set should not contradict the essence of these statements.

- A *mission statement* is a written document that sets out the reason for the existence of the business; that is, its fundamental reason for being.
- A *vision statement* is a written document outlining the broad direction the business hopes to take in the future.
- A *value statement* is a written document that outlines what is most important to the business in terms of values and ethics.

The primary objective of all businesses is to make a profit; however, there can be many other objectives that the business is trying to achieve. Here are some of the most common.

1.2.1 To make a profit

Profit is the amount of money left when the business's expenses are deducted from its revenue. Businesses aim to not only make a profit, but to increase it from year to year. This can be the same objective for the local fish and chip shop to a large business such as Wesfarmers. It is also true of social enterprises, but the difference is where the profit is directed.

1.2.2 To increase market share

In really competitive markets, businesses are constantly trying to increase their share of the **customer** base. **Market share** is the percentage of sales that one business has compared with its competitors in the same industry. Supermarkets, banks and fast-food businesses are good examples of businesses that are constantly trying to increase their market share.

1.2.3 To improve efficiency

Efficiency is the process of making the best possible use of resources. Resources can be categorised as natural, labour and capital, and all are a cost for businesses. An efficient business will ensure that resources are not wasted – that they are used to their maximum potential. You will see examples of this in Unit 3 Area of Study 2 where human resource managers will train employees and manage their performance to ensure that they are working efficiently, as well as in Unit 3 Area of Study 3 where operations managers will implement strategies to ensure that waste is minimised, materials are used efficiently through planning and lean practices are employed.

1.2.4 To improve effectiveness

Effectiveness is the process of achieving all stated goals and objectives. If managers find that only some of their objectives are being achieved, then they have not been totally effective. This extends to what is stated in the mission, vision and value statements as well. There may also be key performance indicator (KPI) targets that have been set. Effective businesses are those that meet or exceed their KPIs. (See Chapters 4 and 5 for more on this topic.)

1.2.5 To fulfil a market need

Businesses are sometimes developed because there is a gap in the market where there is demand for products, but limited supply (**market need**). An example of this has come about because Australia has an ageing population. Housing developers are moving into the development of retirement villages to meet the needs of the large group that is, and will soon be, at the retirement stage of their lives.

1.2.6 To fulfil a social need

Social enterprises in particular are often developed to meet a **social need**. While they make and/or sell goods or provide services for which they charge, the money earned for their activities is used to support causes. The Thankyou movement is one of the best examples of this, where the money they make goes towards providing water, food or hygiene products and training for those in need.

1.2.7 To meet shareholder expectations

Shareholders (see Table 1.2) only invest in companies if they are happy with their performance. If they are not satisfied, they can simply sell their shares. Some people, for example, will only invest in ethical firms. Other people will only invest in those that have a reliable track record of steady growth. Businesses need to meet the expectations of their shareholders, or they risk losing them.

1.3   Stakeholders

1.3.1 Stakeholder types and their interests

Stakeholders are those who have a vested interest in a business, or those who could be affected by decisions made by the owners or managers of the business. Table 1.2 shows examples of stakeholders, but keep in mind that there could be many other groups that would be considered to be stakeholders – and these would vary considerably depending on the type of business, its location and many other factors. Examples include unions and competing businesses.

Stakeholder	Definition	Interests
Owners	Those who own the businesses. More common in structures such as sole traders and partnerships, although also in private companies.	Owners have invested their own money into their businesses; therefore, they want to see it succeed. If they established a social enterprise, then they may be less concerned with making money than with the benefits that can be generated for the wider community. In many cases, however, the owners are in business simply to make a living; therefore, profit is a priority.
Managers	Those in charge of sections of an organisation.	To perform their roles well, leading to the achievement of the organisation's goals. They would want the organisation to be successful so that it continues to operate. They may be entitled to bonuses if the business meets performance targets and makes a significant profit.
Employees	The workers in an organisation. If you are writing about employees, it can be beneficial to make it clear which ones/ roles you are discussing; for example: 'the truck drivers …' or 'the waiters …' In large organisations that employ people in diverse positions, the effect of decisions on each person could be vastly different.	To perform their duties well so that they keep their jobs and may be able to pursue career paths and gain promotions.
Customers	People or businesses who purchase the goods and/or services that are made by the organisation.	To continue to be able to purchase products at the price and quality that they have become used to.
Suppliers	People or businesses who provide the goods and/or services that are demanded by other businesses. *Note: If you are using suppliers as an example in a SAC or exam answer, make sure you say what they supply; for example: suppliers of the cleaning products.*	To see the organisation increase its sales, so that more products will need to be supplied to it, earning greater profit for the **supplier**.
General community	People and groups who may live in areas near the business location or those who may be affected by its business operations.	Interests of a 'general community' can be quite varied depending on what makes them a stakeholder. If they happen to live near the business, then their interests might be in terms of employment opportunities, levels of pollution emissions or even how much support the business provides for the local football and netball teams.

TABLE 1.2 Stakeholder types and their interests

CHAPTER 1

1.3.2 Conflict between stakeholders

In some instances, there can be conflict between the interests of stakeholder groups. An example of this might be employees of a public transport company, with the backing of their union and the Fair Work Commission, seeking a pay rise. The shareholders might be against such a decision because it might reduce the amount of money available to be paid out in dividends. There could also be conflict with the customers if industrial action such as strikes causes inconvenience to their travel plans.

Stakeholders can also have differing viewpoints on corporate social responsibility considerations. While the fundamental objective of businesses is to make a profit, at some stage questions may be asked about the morality of the methods used to pursue this priority. Some shareholders will only invest in companies that are considered to operate in an ethical manner. Some employees will only apply for jobs in organisations that demonstrate corporate social responsibility. For others, these considerations do not matter as much. There may be conflict with some shareholders and employees if the managers pursue profit at all costs, especially if ethical practices are not always followed.

> **Hint**
> Keep it current! Learn more about companies on the ASIC website
> (https://asic.gov.au/online-services/search-asic-s-registers/companies-and-organisations/).

> **Hint**
> The Body Shop Australia has a great deal of information on their corporate social responsibility (CSR) on their website's 'About us' page
> (https://www.thebodyshop.com/en-au/about-us/a/a00001).

1.4 Management styles and skills

1.4.1 Management styles

Managers employ a style when it comes to their decision-making and their relationships with their employees. The style that is used will usually depend on a number of factors, such as the:

- nature of the task
- time that is available
- experience and skill levels of the employees
- manager's preference.

This list contains what we call situational variables; that is, the factors that can change and impact the style that a manager chooses to adopt. It is essential to ensure that the style employed by the manager is appropriate by taking the variables in the list into consideration.

istock.com/PeopleImages

> **Hint**
> If asked to select a **management style** in an exam question, look for the situational variables in the information that is provided to assist in your choice. To identify a style of management (see Table 1.3), look first at who is making the decisions and whether or not they are involving others in the process.

Name of management style	Features	Strengths	Weaknesses
Autocratic	• Manager makes decisions alone • Authority is centralised • Communication is one-way from the manager down • Task-oriented	• Fast • Often clear directions are given • Works well in a crisis situation where time is short and immediate action is required	• No opportunity for input from workers • Workers may resent being ordered around, leading to decreased morale and productivity
Persuasive	• Manager makes decisions alone, but explains why • Authority is centralised • One-way communication • Task-oriented	• Fast • Suits situations where the decision to be made is at a high level and does not require discussion; for example, if a branch of a business is to be shut down, workers will be informed and the reasons will be explained, but workers will not be involved in making the decision	• No opportunity for input from workers • Again, there is the chance that workers will feel alienated, and will not take ownership of decisions that have been made
Consultative	• Manager makes decisions alone, after consulting with staff • Authority is still centralised, but workers are considered • Two-way communication • Slightly more people-oriented	• Workers' opinions may lead to a better decision being made • Workers may take ownership of the decision if they have been involved in the process • Works well in most large-scale organisations; hence, it is probably the most common management style in medium to large businesses	• Can be time-consuming if all stakeholders are consulted • Workers may still feel alienated if they are consulted but their opinions are not incorporated into the final decision
Participative	• Manager and employees make decisions together • Authority is decentralised • Two-way communication • People-oriented	• Can boost morale if workers feel that they are a real part of the process, leading to an increase in productivity • High levels of ownership as workers make decisions themselves • Works well for middle- or lower-level decisions, particularly about issues that directly impact the workers	• Can be very time-consuming • Can cause conflict between workers if they have different points of view • Not all workers want to be involved in decision-making; they may resent being part of the process
Laissez-faire Note: While you might recognise this style in use, think carefully before recommending it as a suitable style	• Employees are left to make decisions on their own in their area • Authority is totally decentralised • Communication channels can vary depending on the organisation	• Workers experience a great deal of control; therefore, it can lead to boosts in morale and productivity • Can be a good style in workplaces where creative freedom is important	• The lack of monitoring from management can lead to problems in terms of control • Some workers may not be capable of this level of self-direction

TABLE 1.3 Characteristics of management styles

CHAPTER 1

> **Hint**
>
> **Contingency approach** (also known as the situational approach) is not a style of management, but is a way of using the styles. This approach means that the manager selects the most appropriate style according to the situation with which they are faced. It should not be recommended if you are asked to identify or suggest a suitable management style.

1.4.2 Management skills

No matter what level or type of manager, there are some common skills that all managers should have. The following **management skills** are listed in the Study Design:

- **communication skills**
- **delegation skills**
- **planning skills**
- **leadership skills**
- **decision-making skills**
- **interpersonal skills**.

Communication skills

- Communication is a two-way process of effectively sending and receiving information.
- Without clear communication, messages can be misunderstood. It's not just about being able to write policies or issue instructions to employees. Effective managers know the importance of listening and of non-verbal communication such as body language.

Delegation skills

- Delegating means passing authority or specific tasks to more junior staff members while still maintaining responsibility.
- This is not about fobbing off undesirable tasks to others! Delegation can be effective to build up skills and confidence in employees. It can also be effective during particularly busy times at the business to ensure deadlines are met.

Planning skills

- Planning skills involve determining achievable goals or objectives within a specified timeframe.
- There are three main categories of planning based on the time period involved and the level of management that is responsible for them (see Table 1.4). Medium to large businesses often have several levels of managers in their structures. Each level of management would have different planning responsibilities.
- The consequences of making a bad strategic plan are much more severe than making a bad operational decision because the impact on the business will be more widespread over a longer time period.
- In a small business, the manager is often the owner and would be responsible for all levels of planning.

Type of planning	Time period and examples	Who is responsible in medium to large businesses
Strategic planning	• Long term, maybe up to five years • Deciding whether to open new branches • Deciding whether to merge with or acquire another business	Senior managers such as managing directors or chief executive officers
Tactical planning	• Short term, from about six months to one or two years • Seasonal buying for retail outlets • Production runs • Anticipating staffing needs of the business	Middle managers, including managers such as human resource or operations managers
Operational planning	• Very short term, even daily planning • Ordering stock • Weekly rosters	Lower managers, frontline managers or supervisors

TABLE 1.4 Features of the three main categories of planning strategies

Leadership skills

- Leadership is the process of influencing workers so that they want to do their best to achieve business objectives.
- Leaders are much more than just managers. They often have inspirational qualities that allow them to share a vision with others. This generates loyalty, creates a positive culture and raises morale.

Decision-making skills

- Effective decision-making requires the ability to select the best course of action from a range of options.
- Managers cannot be effective if they are unable to make decisions. These decisions need to be well informed, consistent and supportive of the mission and strategic plan of the business. There is also an expectation that decisions will reflect an ethical stance to complement the business's corporate social responsibility policies.

Planning or decision-making model

- Whenever plans or decisions have to be made, managers may choose to follow a step model/process (see Table 1.5). This helps to ensure that they are making the best possible plan for the organisation.

Step one
Identify the issue that requires a decision or the course of action that requires a plan.
It is good to be clear about precisely why any planning or decision is required. What is the objective to be achieved?
Step two
Conduct a SWOT analysis (see the next page).
The SWOT analysis will help to determine possible avenues to pursue and will clarify options available.
Step three
Based on the results of the SWOT analysis, devise a number of planning options or possible decisions.
If possible, several options could be developed that might fulfil the needs of the business.
Step four
Select the best option and implement it.
The implementation phase will vary in time depending on the nature of the plan, the type of business and a number of other factors.
Step five
Monitor this plan or the results of the decision and evaluate the effectiveness.
This stage is very important. It can be useful to go back to Step one to be reminded about why the plan or decision needed to be made in the first place. The evaluation should be based on this information.
Step six
If it is not proving to be an adequate plan, go back and select another option from Step three.
Perhaps another plan will be more effective. Maybe the decision was flawed. If the step model was followed, then there should be other options ready to try.

TABLE 1.5 Steps in a planning or decision-making model

SWOT analysis

SWOT stands for strengths, weaknesses, opportunities and threats. Conducting a SWOT analysis is standard practice in many businesses, particularly as part of planning and decision-making processes. Managers would take note of the following.

- Strengths: What is working well in the current situation? This is especially relevant to the internal and operating environments.

- Weaknesses: What is not working well in the current situation? This also applies to the internal and operating environments.

- Opportunities: Are there potential chances for success in the future? These opportunities may come from any of the three environments: internal, operating and/or macro.

- Threats: Are there potential forces that could prevent success in the future? If the threats come from the internal or operating environments, there is the possibility that they can be avoided; but if the threats are from the macro environment, they may be inevitable.

Interpersonal skills

- Interpersonal skills involve the ability to relate to and empathise with others and build effective relationships.

- Interpersonal skills link considerably with leadership skills, as it would be difficult to be a good leader without interpersonal skills. It can be invaluable when trying to overcome employee resistance to change (see Chapter 5).

1.4.3 Relationship between styles and skills

The style of management that is embraced by a manager will often reflect their own skill levels and competency in certain areas. Those with interpersonal skills will find it easier to successfully use a participative management style. Managers who are poor at decision-making would find it difficult to use the autocratic, persuasive or even the consultative management styles. Communication skills are vital for all managers, but in the autocratic and persuasive styles, the receiving aspect tends not to be used. They still need to be able to express themselves clearly when issuing instructions.

1.5 Corporate culture

1.5.1 Corporate culture – official and real

Corporate culture is the shared values, beliefs and behaviours of the people within a business. The **official corporate culture** is an outline of the preferred values, beliefs and behaviours of the people within a business as stated in official documents such as the company motto or mission statement. The **real corporate culture** reflects how things actually operate. This may be the same as the official culture, or may be totally different if there are issues that have not been resolved.

The desired corporate culture can be quite different depending on the nature of the business. A bank, for example, may try to generate a formal culture where confidentiality and reserved behaviours are expected. A café located in a hipster area of Melbourne, on the other hand, may aim for a casual, informal culture. While both the café and the bank may aim to have professional staff, the nature of the different jobs and the expectations of their customers can result in very different cultures developing. Even if a business is small, it still needs to have a positive corporate culture. Some businesses may state that their culture is based on ethical practices, but employees may be aware that that is not the case. Where the real and official cultures differ, tensions can occur that are difficult to resolve.

1.5.2 Importance of corporate culture

Managers are becoming increasingly aware of the importance of corporate culture, so much so that they look for ways to create a positive atmosphere in the workplace. The benefits of a positive corporate culture for a business can be:

- better staff retention rates
- attractiveness to new employees, allowing the business to select from the best in their fields
- increased productivity, leading to greater success.

What makes a good corporate culture?

There have been many studies looking at what makes a good corporate culture. In *Building a winning culture*, Bain & Company highlights attributes of winning corporate cultures such as: instilling in employees a desire to win; creating a situation where the employees put themselves in the shoes of the business owners when making decisions; focusing not only on the internal aspects, but also those that relate to customers, competitors and the local **community**; being prepared to act; prioritising teamwork within the business; and ensuring that the business resonates with passion and energy.

1.5.3 Indicators of corporate culture

Indicators of corporate culture are the aspects of the business that outsiders can view to gauge what sort of culture exists and whether it is what is desired.

- *Communication channels*: Are they formal or informal? Are employees encouraged to seek out managers to discuss issues? The manner in which communication occurs can reflect the formality of the business.

- *Dress of employees*: This depends somewhat on whether there are requirements for staff in terms of expectations of dress or a uniform. The culture of the business can be seen in the way that people choose to dress within these policies or expectations. If there is a uniform that employees refuse to wear, or wear inappropriately, it may reflect dissatisfaction of staff and a poor culture. If, on the other hand, employees dress appropriately (whether that means wearing uniforms correctly or dressing casually), it may reflect a positive culture. The way people dress can often have an effect on the way they act and their levels of productivity.

- *The willingness to achieve*: Some workplaces have a culture of trying as hard as possible to be the best in their field, while in others the attitude is quite relaxed (even slack!). A positive culture is often shown in workplaces where employees are happy to work hard.

- *Socialisation*: Do the staff mingle? Do they get along with each other? This can be seen in small ways such as whether they stop and have lunch together or whether they continue to work throughout their lunch breaks, eating at their desks. Do they celebrate birthdays or have Christmas parties? While some workplaces may not value too much socialisation, it is generally agreed that some form of bonding can generate effective working relationships, where bullying and harassment is seldom seen.

> **Hint**
>
> Make sure you have a list of adjectives to describe different types of corporate culture; 'good' and 'bad' don't really say much at all. Here are a few to get you started:
>
> - positive   - bullying
> - industrious   - supportive.
> - fearful

Glossary

autocratic management style The style where the manager makes all decisions alone, with centralised authority and one-way communication.

business objectives Goals that the owners and/or managers of a business hope to achieve.

communication skills A two-way process of effectively sending and receiving information.

community A group of people who live near each other, or have something in common.

consultative management style The style where the manager makes the final decision after gaining feedback from stakeholders, authority is still somewhat centralised and communication is a two-way process.

contingency or situational approach A strategy where the manager selects the style according to the situation with which they are faced.

corporate culture The shared values, beliefs and behaviours of the people in an organisation.

customers Those who purchase goods and/or services from a business.

decision-making skills The ability to select the best course of action from a range of options.

delegation skills Passing authority for specific tasks to more junior staff members.

effectiveness The process of achieving all stated goals and objectives.

efficiency The process of making the best possible use of resources.

employee A worker in a business who is paid an income in exchange for their labour.

government business enterprises (GBEs) Organisations that still belong to the public sector but have the overriding objective of making a profit.

interpersonal skills The ability to relate to and empathise with others and build effective relationships.

laissez-faire management style The style where managers allow employees to take full responsibility for decisions within their areas; authority is decentralised.

leadership skills The ability to influence and inspire workers so that they want to achieve organisational objectives.

A+ DIGITAL FLASHCARDS
Revise this topic's key terms and concepts by scanning the QR code or typing the URL into your browser.

https://get.ga/aplus-vce-busmgmt-u34

management skills The abilities that benefit managers to perform their roles.

management style The preferred method of operating as a manager, including ways of making decisions and inclusiveness of employees.

managers Those in leadership positions who have responsibility for a section of a business.

market need A gap where products desired by consumers are not being supplied by businesses.

market share The percentage of sales or business that one firm has compared with its competitors in the same industry.

official corporate culture The preferred culture that is stated in official documents such as mission statements.

owners People who have bought and/or established their own businesses.

participative management style The style where the manager encourages employees to become actively involved in the decision-making process, authority is decentralised and communication is a two-way process.

partnership A business structure where up to 20 people own and run a business together.

persuasive management style The style where the manager makes decisions alone but explains the reasons to employees, authority is centralised and communication is one-way.

planning skills The ability to determine achievable goals or objectives within a specified timeframe.

private company A business that has up to 50 shareholders and is not listed on the stock exchange.

profit The amount of income left over when expenses are deducted from revenue.

public company A business that can have any number of shareholders and is listed on the stock exchange.

real corporate culture The corporate culture as it is demonstrated by the people in the workplace. This may be the same as the official culture or could be quite different.

shareholder Those who have invested money in a business, hoping to earn dividends and increase the value of their shares.

social enterprise A business that provides goods and/or services to earn money that funds a social cause.

social need A gap in the market where products (goods or services) that would benefit society are not being produced.

sole trader A structure where one person owns the business.

stakeholders Those who have an interest in an organisation, or those who could be affected by decisions made by the business.

suppliers Those who provide the goods and/or services that are required by other businesses.

Revision summary

The first column in the table below has the key knowledge points of Unit 3 Area of Study 1. Read the suggestions in the second column for ways that you can complete notes that will be useful for preparation for both School-assessed Coursework tasks as well as your end-of-year exam.

Unit 3 Area of Study 1 Business foundations	Suggestions for summary notes
Types of businesses including: • sole traders • partnerships • private limited companies • public listed companies • social enterprises • government business enterprises	Define all terms and list an example of each.
Business objectives including: • to make a profit • to increase market share • to improve efficiency • to improve effectiveness • to fulfil a market need • to fulfil a social need • to meet shareholder expectations	Provide an example for each of these objectives. Make sure you understand why businesses may want to achieve these and why different types of businesses may prioritise some objectives more than others.
Stakeholders of businesses including: • owners • managers • employees • customers • suppliers • the general community	Be able to define 'stakeholder' as well as each of the stakeholder examples listed here.
Characteristics of stakeholders of businesses including: • their interests • potential conflicts between stakeholders	• Make a list of stakeholders of one of the businesses that you studied, clearly stating what their interest in the business is. • Make sure you can clearly explain how there might be conflict between stakeholders.
Management styles including: • autocratic • persuasive • consultative • participative • laissez-faire	• Define all styles; include at least two characteristics, one of which must relate to decision-making. • List one strength and one weakness for each style.
The appropriateness of management styles in relation to: • the nature of the task • time • experience of employees • manager preference	It's important to remember that not every style is appropriate in every situation. Try to come up with a situation for each of these and state the appropriate style or styles. Or suggest styles that would not be appropriate and state why.

››

» Management skills including: • communication • delegation • planning • leadership • decision-making • interpersonal	• Define the skills. • Consider the Australian and global business case studies that you looked at in class. Note which of the skills were demonstrated by the managers in these businesses. Also note any skill deficiencies that were apparent. • If you do not have case studies from class, then consider the managers in your workplace if you have a part-time job.
The relationship between management styles and management skills	A quick way to revise this is to list the management styles, then next to each one list two skills that would be essential to operate within the style.
Corporate culture, both official and real	Define 'corporate culture', 'real corporate culture' and 'official corporate culture'. In addition, list some of the indicators of culture and words that can be used to describe culture.

VCE Business Management Study Design 2023–2027 p. 17, © VCAA 2022

Exam practice

Solutions for this section start on page 96.

Question 1 (2 marks) ●●○

Outline one advantage and one disadvantage of setting up a partnership compared with operating as a sole trader (sole proprietor).

Question 2 (1 mark) ●○○

State the main objective of establishing a social enterprise.

Question 3 (2 marks) ●●○

Outline two differences between a private company and a public company.

Question 4 (4 marks) ●○○

Explain the interests of two different stakeholders of a hairdressing salon that operates as a sole proprietor.

Question 5 (2 marks) ●●○

'Corporate social responsibility is only important for large businesses.' Explain if this statement is true or false.

Question 6 (2 + 2 = 4 marks) ●●○

Suggest an appropriate management style for each of the following situations.

a   A frontline manager in a large hotel must organise the next month's work rosters.

b   Senior managers are looking at expanding the business overseas within the next 5 years.

Question 7 (2 marks) ●●○

Why is the laissez-faire management style not appropriate for most large businesses?

Question 8 (2 marks) ●○○

What is the difference between interpersonal skills and communication skills?

Question 9 (2 marks) ●●○

Explain why a manager with good decision-making skills might find that the consultative style of management works well.

Question 10 (4 marks) ●●●

'The autocratic management style is inappropriate in the modern world.' Is there any truth in this statement? Explain.

Question 11 (2 marks) ●○○

Distinguish between real and official corporate culture.

Question 12 (4 marks) ●●○

Explain two benefits of having a positive corporate culture.

Question 13 (3 marks) ●●●

Bain & Company suggest that having an external focus on customers, competitors and the community can be an important aspect of corporate culture in a business. Explain why an external focus could be beneficial.

Question 14 (4 marks) ●●●

'Recruitment can be vital when trying to develop a positive corporate culture.' Discuss this statement.

Question 15 (4 marks) ○○■

Explain why small businesses need positive corporate cultures as much as large businesses.

Question 16 (2 marks) ©VCAA 2017 SA Q1b ○○■

Outline **one** reason why a business may choose to operate as a partnership rather than as a sole trader.

Question 17 (2 marks) ©VCAA 2018 SA Q1a ○■■

Define the term 'partnership' as a type of business.

Question 18 (5 marks) ©VCAA 2018 SB Q5 ○○○

Use the case study below to outline the interests of **two** relevant stakeholders of Ocean Skate Hub. Explain how these interests may be in conflict.

The *Daily Swell* is a local print and online newspaper. It recently published the following article about a local business.

CASE STUDY

Regional community hub for all

Tessa Adams and Charlie Liu opened Ocean Skate Hub in 2017. It is a social enterprise aimed at servicing the needs of the local youth community. It offers indoor and outdoor skate parks, and youth and homework clubs. It also operates a sports shop and café.

After finishing school, Charlie completed a Sports Management degree and Tessa completed a Commerce degree. Having both worked in their chosen fields for several years, Tessa and Charlie recently moved from the city back to their hometown, where they began setting up their business enterprise. Charlie commented that 'we wanted to offer a place where young people from the community could come and try different activities, socialise and gain some new skills'.

After carrying out their research into what financial assistance was available, Tessa and Charlie applied for support through a government initiative called Social Enterprise Finance Australia (SEFA).

SEFA provides finance solutions to mission-led organisations and is deeply committed to fostering positive social and environmental impacts in communities across Australia. SEFA is also there to help new business ventures, like Ocean Skate Hub, build their capacity to manage debt and become financially sustainable.

'We highly value the intensive support we received from SEFA. They helped us put together a rock-solid business case', said Tessa.

Ocean Skate Hub uses its website and social media to provide information to customers and has launched an app to let members book activity sessions. Members are encouraged to give feedback to the organisation to help it meet its aims of improving customer service and finding interesting activities for all users.

All employees are from the local area, and Tessa and Charlie are passionate about keeping all services within the region. Their preference is for staff training to be carried out within the business; however, this is proving to be challenging for Ocean Skate Hub to achieve, and Tessa and Charlie feel they may have to outsource staff training in the future.

With the success of the business behind them, Tessa and Charlie have big plans for expansion in 2019 to provide services for the whole community, not just its youth. These include IT classes for the elderly, as well as photography, cooking, woodwork and gardening classes for all ages.

'With all these exciting changes planned for 2019, we will be relaunching as "Ocean Hub" to better reflect the expanded range of community activities that will soon be available', Charlie said.

Mayor Colin Sprey commented that 'it is encouraging to see our young entrepreneurs giving back to their community'.

Question 19 (2 marks)   ©VCAA   2020 SA Q1a

In 2017, John was employed as the manager of a bakery with 80 employees. In 2020, the business has had the following business objectives:

- to increase profits by 10%
- to reduce staff absenteeism by 20%.

John has adopted an autocratic management style.

Define the term 'business objective'.

Question 20 (5 marks)   ©VCAA   2020 SA Q1b   ●●

Evaluate the suitability of the management style John has adopted for achieving the bakery's business objectives.

Exam practice: Case study

Solutions for this section start on page 99.

CASE STUDY | The town of Dango attracts a large number of tourists, especially in winter because it is located near the ski fields of Mt Hotham and Falls Creek. The town has two cafés, which are fiercely competitive. They are Kath's Café, which is owned by Kathryn Mortimer as a sole trader, and Frost, which is owned by brother and sister Tony and Anne Norts in a partnership. Both cafés open at 7 am and close at 5 pm, 7 days a week. Both cafés employ five people in part-time positions. Kathryn believes in managing her employees in a consultative manner. Anne is quite autocratic, while Tony believes that the only way to successfully manage staff is to adopt a participative approach.

Questions

Question 1 (2 marks)   ●○○

Define 'market share' and provide an example.

Question 2 (4 marks)   ●●

Discuss whether sole traders or partnerships are better forms of ownership for a café.

Question 3 (4 marks)   ●●

Identify and explain two stakeholders of Frost who could have conflicting interests.

Question 4 (2 marks)   ●○○

Explain one skill that Kathryn would need to be an effective consultative manager.

Question 5 (6 marks)   ●●●

Evaluate whether having one autocratic and one participative manager is likely to work effectively.

Question 6 (2 marks)   ●●

Define 'corporate culture' and propose one reason why it is important for a café.

Total = 20 marks

Chapter 2
Area of Study 2: Human resource management

Area of Study summary

The title of this area of study says it all. Human resources are people, so this is where you will learn about how to effectively manage the people in a business. Recruitment is covered in Unit 2 Area of Study 2, so here we start with a scenario in which the business is fully staffed.

First, you need to be able to link back to the business objectives that were covered in the previous area of study. You will then be provided with a number of theories and strategies that a human resource manager could implement to help them to achieve the objectives. These include motivation, training and performance management strategies.

You will also learn about the different reasons why someone might terminate their employment and the options that are available to a human resource manager to deal with this situation.

Finally, even in the best-managed businesses, disputes can sometimes arise. If the dispute is about pay or conditions of work, then it is 'workplace' relations. You will learn about the players in this field and the different ways that disputes can be resolved.

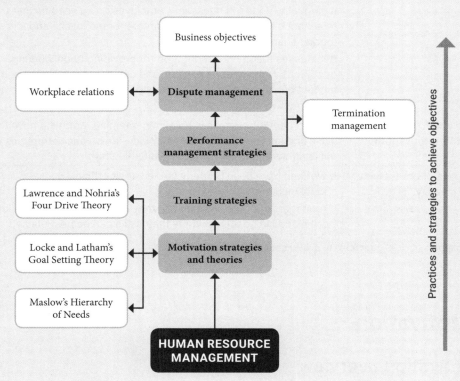

Area of Study 2 Outcome 2

On completing this outcome you should be able to:

- explain theories of **motivation** and apply them to a range of contexts, and analyse and evaluate strategies related to the management of employees.

The key skills demonstrated in this outcome are:

- identify, define, describe and apply business management concepts and terms
- interpret, discuss, compare and evaluate business information, theories and ideas
- analyse case studies and contemporary examples of management
- apply business management knowledge to practical and/or simulated business situations
- propose, justify and evaluate management strategies to improve business performance.

VCE Business Management Study Design 2023–2027 p. 18, © VCAA 2022

2.1 Human resource management (HRM)

2.1.1 HRM overview

Whether a business has 5 or 500 employees, the business owners and/or managers need to ensure that they are managed well. Employees (the **human resources**) will not be productive if they feel unappreciated or have to endure poor work conditions. **Human resource management (HRM)** is the management of workplace tasks that relate to the employment, retention and termination of employees.

2.1.2 HRM and business objectives

There are a number of **strategies** related to managing employees that can be implemented to achieve **business objectives**. These are set out in Table 2.1.

Business objectives	Examples of HRM strategies that can help to achieve business objectives
Increase profit	Managers need to ensure that wages are appropriate and not too expensive.
Increase market share	Well-trained employees will deliver good customer service or will create high-quality goods. If necessary, employees may need further training to enhance their skills, leading to greater brand loyalty and increased market share. Businesses that have a reputation for providing good working conditions, training opportunities and career paths will attract the highest-quality applicants when recruiting. This also gives the business a competitive edge.
Retain skilled employees and reduce the staff turnover rate	The recruitment process is costly, so retaining staff who have the required skills and knowledge is essential. Work–life balance strategies could assist in attracting and retaining valuable staff.
Increase the rate of productivity, and hence efficiency	If workers have been properly trained, their efficiency levels should increase. If managers conduct skills audits, they can then ensure that workers have been placed in positions where their skills can be best utilised.

TABLE 2.1 Examples of HRM strategies to achieve business objectives

2.2 Motivation

2.2.1 Motivation overview

Many of the strategies in Table 2.1 rely on increasing the motivation levels of employees. **Motivation** can be defined as the practices or factors that drive a person to perform at their best.

There have been many studies of motivation resulting in theories that can be applied to the workplace; however, the underlying philosophies of these theories may be different.

- Needs-based theories work on the principle that the satisfaction of needs leads to motivation. An example of this is Maslow's theory.

- Goal-setting theories work on the principle that the achievement of goals gives a sense of satisfaction that is motivational. An example of this is the theory developed by Locke and Latham.

- Contingency theories attempt to explain and understand the process by which motivation occurs. An example of this is the Four Drive Theory by Lawrence and Nohria.

  Each of these theories is explained further in the next few sections.

2.2.2 Maslow's Hierarchy of Needs

Abraham Maslow (1908–1970) was an American psychologist who created a hierarchy of needs (see Figure 2.1). He believed that people progress through stages as they mature and develop.

FIGURE 2.1 Maslow's Hierarchy of Needs

Maslow's Hierarchy of Needs states that a person is unlikely to move to the next level of needs until the former one has been achieved; that is, that people cannot skip the levels of need.

1 Physiological needs: We start with the basic survival needs of food, water and so on. In the workplace, these translate to being paid fairly and having decent work conditions.

2 Safety and security needs: This stage develops once our basic needs have been addressed. As a child, this might mean the security of knowing where our parents are and a general feeling of safety at home. As adults, this might translate into job security including having a permanent appointment or long-term contract, having a workplace that abides by occupational health and safety legislation and having a reasonable amount of superannuation.

3 Belonging needs: Children start to form friendships when they reach this level. Adults might join clubs or play team sports. In the workplace, this could mean being involved in team-based projects, socialisation events or simply identifying with the culture of the business.

4 Esteem needs: Esteem is achieved at two levels: the first is the esteem in which others hold us; the second is self-esteem or self-respect. In the workplace, this can become apparent as workers strive to be recognised for achievements and take on projects that will enhance their own self-esteem if performed well.

5 Self-actualisation needs: Once all the previous needs have been addressed, there is the opportunity to achieve the final level, although Maslow made it clear that very few actually reach and maintain this stage. People who reach this stage display some of the following characteristics.

   – They enjoy deep relationships.

   – They accept themselves and others.

   – They have a sense of humility.

   – They can be creative and original.

   – They have strong ethics.

In the workplace, these are the people who have no further needs. They have achieved all that they want to in their careers and don't yearn for anything to realise satisfaction at work.

HRM using Maslow's theory

Modern human resource managers could use aspects of Maslow's theory when trying to motivate workers. They would need to be aware that the employees will be at different stages of development; therefore, a range of strategies might need to be applied.

Some workers may be at the 'belonging' stage, so a team-building weekend might work really well with them. Others may have reached the 'esteem' level, so they will respond well to recognition of their achievements.

2.2.3 Locke and Latham's Goal Setting Theory

Edwin A. Locke and Gary Latham have published many books and articles on the concept of goal setting, its relationship with motivation and their **Goal Setting Theory**. Locke and Latham's research showed that specific and challenging or difficult goals led to better task performance than vague or easy goals.

Specific goals

Goals need to be specific so that the information is clear, allowing less room for error and individual interpretation.

Challenging goals

Goals need to be challenging or difficult because people tend to exert more effort and try harder to attain more difficult goals. Of course, the goals should be set so that they are achievable; therefore, they also need to be realistic.

In addition to this, Locke and Latham state there are moderator variables, which have the ability to strengthen or weaken the effects that are possible from goal setting.

Moderator variables

- Ability: Employees should have the ability to achieve the goal. It must be possible to attain.
- Performance feedback: Feedback is essential to increase performance. It can assist in letting the employee know if more effort is required or whether they should try a different way of approaching the task.
- Goal commitment: Success is only possible if the person is really dedicated to achieving the goal.
- Task complexity: The task that is set to achieve the goal must be straightforward so that people feel able to complete it.
- Situational constraints/resources: People need the information and materials to complete their tasks.
- Personality: While personality can have an effect, the structure provided by clear goal setting can override individual differences in personality.
- Goals and effect: If goals are set effectively, they can lead to increased satisfaction, less boredom and more interest in the task.

The process of goal setting

Locke and Latham stated that there are seven key steps involved in goal setting.

1 Specify the general objective or tasks to be done.
2 Specify how the performance in question will be measured.
3 Specify the standard or target to be reached.
4 Specify the time span involved.
5 Prioritise goals.
6 Optional step: rate goals as to difficulty and importance.
7 Determine coordination requirements (with other people).

By following these steps, the goals should be such that they meet the requirements in terms of being both specific and challenging, hence leading to a better chance of being motivational. Motivation occurs when people experience a sense of achievement from having accomplished their goals and completed the task that was set for them.

HRM using Locke and Latham's Goal Setting Theory

Employees are set goals constantly – some are determined by managers; others may be self-imposed. Managers may be able to better motivate workers by ensuring that the goals set for workers are specific and challenging. This would require sound knowledge of each employee's skills and personal characteristics so that appropriate and achievable goals can be set. With consideration of the moderator variables, including the importance of performance feedback, goal setting should prove to be effective in increasing the motivation levels of employees.

2.2.4 Lawrence and Nohria's Four Drive Theory

The **Four Drive Theory** is quite different from the previous two theories. This theory is based on the concept of 'drives' that, according to Lawrence and Nohria, exist in all of us. The four drives are interrelated, and some will be of more importance than others to different people.

The four drives are as follows.

- *The drive to acquire*: While this relates to remuneration, it could also be satisfied with high-status positions or recognition of achievements.

- *The drive to bond*: This drive relates to wanting to form long-term relationships within the business and to feel supported and included.

- *The drive to learn*: The third drive relates to people's desire to continually learn new things and increase their ability to comprehend the world around them.

- *The drive to defend*: The final drive relates to our feeling the need to defend ourselves and those for whom we care. In a business setting, this could be linked to defending an employee's position within the workplace or defending people in their department if criticised. This drive is slightly different from the previous three in that it is unlikely to be activated unless there is a challenge or threat.

HRM using Lawrence and Nohria's Four Drive Theory

Identifying the primary drives of employees will allow a manager to more quickly provide the situations or resources that could allow the workers to become satisfied and motivated. In some cases, more than one need can be satisfied at the same time. For example, if employees are given the responsibility to conduct a research project in a team, it may go towards satisfying the drive to bond as well as the drive to learn.

> **Hint**
>
> To find out more about Locke and Latham's and Lawrence and Nohria's motivation theories, read their books on the subject:
> - Locke, EA & Latham, GP. (1984) *Goal Setting: A Motivational Theory That Works*. Prentice Hall, Englewood Cliffs, New Jersey.
> - Locke, EA & Latham, GP. (1990) *A Theory of Goal Setting and Task Performance*. Prentice Hall, Englewood Cliffs, New Jersey.
> - Locke, EA & Latham, GP. (eds) (2013) *New Developments in Goal Setting and Task Performance*. Routledge/Taylor & Francis Group, New York.
> - Lawrence PR & Nohria N. (2002) *Driven: How Human Nature Shapes Our Choices*. Jossey-Bass, San Francisco.

2.2.5 Comparison of motivation theories

While it is easy to see how the three motivational theories differ, it is important to be aware of the similarities as well. Table 2.2 sets out both.

	Lawrence and Nohria vs Locke and Latham	Maslow vs Lawrence and Nohria	Locke and Latham vs Maslow
Similarities	Setting goals and the motivation felt by the achievement of them can be linked to the drive to acquire (achievement).	Both relate to satisfaction – in M's case, it is needs and in LN's case, it is drives. Both theories were originally written to explain human behaviour, not intended for workplace motivation, although both can be applied to businesses.	Goal setting could lead to Maslow's esteem level being achieved.
Differences	LL = Goal Setting Theory LN = need to satisfy the four drives; therefore, their fundamental approaches to improving motivation are quite different	M has five levels of needs. LN has four drives. M = must progress up through the levels one at a time LN = possible to be working towards more than one drive at the same time	LL = Goal Setting Theory M = satisfying needs one level at a time; therefore, their fundamental approaches to improving motivation are quite different

TABLE 2.2 Comparison of motivation theories

> **Hint**
> Not all motivational theories are equal. If you are faced with a question that asks you to suggest one, then look at the situation that the business is facing. What is lacking? That might help you to select the theory that would be more likely to be effective.

2.2.6 Advantages and disadvantages and effects of motivation

Besides the use of a motivational theory, managers may decide to implement a **motivation strategy** to lift the morale and performance of their employees. Each strategy has associated costs and benefits, and some will be more effective in the short term as opposed to having long-term effects (see Table 2.3).

istock.com/FatCamera

> **Hint**
> Consider the circumstances of the business before suggesting an expensive solution to a lack of motivation among employees. If the business is struggling financially, it is not appropriate to suggest pay increases because the business may not be able to afford them. Make sure your answers are appropriate and relevant to the situation that is described in the question.

Motivation strategy	Advantages	Disadvantages	Short- and long-term effects
Performance-related pay	Employees may strive to work hard knowing that their efforts will be rewarded monetarily. This could be effective with those who have families to support or financial commitments such as a mortgage.	Businesses may not be able to afford the extra payments. Some people are not motivated by money.	This is more likely to have short-term benefits. If the work is not enjoyable or giving employees a sense of achievement, extra money may not be enough in the long run.
Career advancement	This can appeal to those who want a sense of achievement as well as more responsibility. Employees may work hard for several years in anticipation of eventually getting a promotion.	There may be limited opportunities for advancement. Smaller businesses may only have one or two people in management or supervisory positions; therefore, the chance to advance is slim.	This is more likely to have long-term motivational benefits for the business. Employees would need to demonstrate good work habits over an extended period of time before being considered for a promotion.
Investment in training	Better-trained employees feel more confident about their abilities. This can improve the corporate culture and lead to productivity improvements. If it is a service provider, better-trained employees may add to the customer satisfaction levels, resulting in fewer complaints and more repeat customers.	Training can be very expensive for a business. Well-trained employees might resign and take their new skills to another business.	There could be both short- and long-term benefits of greater investment in training. In the short term, the workers' performance is likely to improve. In the long term, employees may be grateful for the improvements in their skill levels and may remain loyal to the business.
Support strategies – this can be in the form of encouragement or even recognition of good work that has been performed	If employees feel out of their depth, they may just need some encouragement and support to motivate them. This is not an expense for the business, but can be very effective to build their confidence to the point where their work performance increases.	There really are no disadvantages of offering support to employees. It is a practice that good managers would use often to motivate their employees.	This can have both short- and long-term benefits for both the business and the employees. As their confidence increases, the employees are improving their performance and they may be willing to undertake more difficult tasks or offer solutions or proposals for new ideas to benefit the business over time.
Sanction strategies – this means a penalty for undesirable behaviour. In a carrot or stick scenario, this is the stick!	This can stop undesirable behaviours quickly. The idea of getting a pay cut or missing out on promotions can get people back on track fast.	It is not going to actually motivate people to want to work harder, which is what motivated employees tend to do. They may stop undesirable practices, but will probably be resentful about the sanctions that are imposed to the point where their work performance may actually be worse.	This is definitely a short-term practice, if it is done at all. The long-term adverse effects will make the situation worse. If a sanction is considered necessary, it would be beneficial to follow it up with a more positive motivational strategy such as offering support or investment in training to gain long-term benefits for both the business and the self-esteem of the employee.

TABLE 2.3 Characteristics of motivation strategies

2.3 Training

2.3.1 Training overview

Training is the process of developing workplace skills. Training may be required right at the start of employment if the person is unfamiliar with machinery or processes used by the business. Even for staff who have been at the workplace for some time, training is always going to be necessary at some stage. Before the training is undertaken, the manager must decide the following.

- Who needs to be trained? Everyone? Or a few core people who can then train the other employees?

- Should the training be done at the organisation or outside; for example, at a training institution?

Training activities

The Australian Industry Group found in 2018 that employers used a variety of methods to ensure that employees had the skills required to perform at a high level in their jobs. While they tried to employ people with the required qualifications and skills, 68% of their measures were to retrain existing staff in new skills. This was a preferred option for many businesses: to employ people with basic skills, then to train them further in ways that reflect the standards and needs of the particular business. (See https://cdn.aigroup.com.au/Reports/2018/Survey_Report_WFDNeeds_Skilling_Sept2018.pdf.)

The *Victorian Skills and Training Employer Survey* in 2015 found that 56% of Victorian workplaces used a type of formal training in the previous year, with more than 25% using VET providers to deliver the training. Almost 40% of the workplaces intended to use TAFEs to deliver VET courses in the following year. (See https://www.education.vic.gov.au/Documents/training/employers/industry/trainingskillssurvey.doc.)

2.3.2 On-the-job versus off-the-job training

On-the-job training occurs while the employee is at work, undertaking their usual tasks. It may consist of a mentor guiding a new staff member or may be more formalised into specific training sessions at the workplace.

Off-the-job training requires the employees to attend a course or training session at another venue. This may just be for a couple of hours or may involve weeks or even months of study at a training facility.

There is now an increasing reliance on online training modules in workplaces. The COVID-19 pandemic increased the rate at which these were rolled out to employees who could no longer attend face-to-face training sessions. It is quite common for employees to complete privacy and workplace health and safety training online every year to ensure that they are up to date with the latest legislation and procedures.

So are these on-the-job or off-the-job training? Really they span both, but are more aligned to on-the-job training, even if they are completed while working at home.

The human resource manager would need to consider the following questions before deciding on the most appropriate form of training.

- If internal training is preferred, is the training going to be provided by someone in-house or by an external provider who comes to the business or provides training online?

- How is the training going to be evaluated?

- Will follow-up training be required at a later date?

There are advantages and disadvantages to both on- and off-the-job training, as can be seen in Table 2.4.

	Advantages	Disadvantages
On the job	• Can be done during normal working hours • Can develop good relationships between employees • Less expensive than an external course	• May not have trainers on staff with the required expertise • There may be distractions with normal work occurring
Off the job	• Can seek out cutting-edge training • Removes normal work distractions • Can give the employee qualifications (e.g. Certificate IV)	• Can be expensive • Can be time-consuming, especially if travel to the training facility is required

TABLE 2.4 Comparison of on-the-job and off-the-job training

2.4 Performance management

2.4.1 Performance management strategies overview

Performance management involves the various methods of achieving the maximum performance levels that are possible from employees. There can be a close link between performance management and motivation. If employees' performances are managed well, it can not only lead to more chance of achieving the business's objectives, but can also assist employees to achieve their own objectives, which may include getting more experience and pursuing a career path.

2.4.2 Management by objectives

Management by objectives (MBO) is a theory that was devised by Peter Drucker in 1954. MBO suggests that managers and employees need to be clear about their objectives before they can pursue any activity. The achievement of the objectives can then be used as criteria to evaluate the success of the employee or manager in conducting their role in the organisation. Two main stages are addressed in MBO.

1 Determine the business's objectives.

2 Plan how to achieve the objectives efficiently and effectively.

2.4.3 Appraisals

Performance appraisals are evaluations of an employee's work over a period of time. Managers may consider the following points when organising and conducting performance appraisals.

- They should occur at regular intervals (12 months is usual, but it could be 6 months, 2 years or any period of time).

- The employee's performance should be measured against their job description, the business's goals and personal goals.

- Feedback should first be gathered from at least the employee's manager/supervisor and also, if possible, from colleagues, customers and/or lower staff. This is sometimes called 360-degree feedback (see Figure 2.2).

- A formal meeting time should be arranged.

FIGURE 2.2 360-degree feedback

- The discussion should remain solely about the performance appraisal.
- It is important to focus on goals for the next time period, not just past performance.
- They can assist in developing career paths.
- There are really two possible outcomes of a performance appraisal.
    - If the performance is found to be unsatisfactory, further training may be recommended – or a reprimand or other negative consequence may follow.
    - If the performance is found to be satisfactory, positive consequences may follow including recognition, promotion, bonuses or even a pay increase.

2.4.4 Self-evaluation

Employees are often aware of their own performance and ways in which to improve it. Giving employees the opportunity to evaluate their work standards can be beneficial and quite empowering. Often this forms the first stage of a more formal appraisal. **Self-evaluations** can give employees the opportunity to document their achievements at the organisation and make suggestions for further training and development that they feel will assist them with their preferred career path. This can be very beneficial for their managers/supervisors as they get an insight into their employees that they may not have had previously.

2.4.5 Employee observation

One way to determine the performance of employees is for managers or peers to observe their performance. These **employee observations** could be anonymous or with the employee knowing that their peers or manager may witness their performance. Often people who provide advice over the phone from call centres will state that the phone call is being recorded for training purposes. Secret shoppers in supermarkets or department stores evaluate employees' customer service and provide feedback that can be useful for their future development.

> **Hint**
> Keep in mind that performance management incorporates performance appraisals. They are not the same thing. Check the definitions of both terms at the end of this chapter to ensure that you know the difference.

2.5 Termination

2.5.1 Termination overview

Employees will eventually leave the business. **Termination** simply means 'the end'. It is not always a negative situation, especially if the employee is retiring or resigning to go to a better job.

> **Hint**
> Be clear about who decides each type of termination. Is it the manager or the employee?

2.5.2 Types of termination

The reasons why employees leave vary, as described in Table 2.5.

Termination type	What it means
Resignation	An employee chooses to leave an organisation. This may be because they have another job to go to or are moving to another area. It is a personal decision made by the employee. In some cases it may be because they are dissatisfied with their current place of employment.
Redundancy – involuntary	The situation in which there is no longer a position for one or more employees; in other words, there are more employees than are needed. The process of the redundancy may be set out in the business's enterprise agreement. This will state the criteria for determining which employees are to be let go first. As the details are in the agreement, these criteria will be different for different businesses. Most employees who are made redundant are entitled to redundancy packages; that is, an amount of money usually based on the number of years' employment at that business.
Redundancy – voluntary	The actual situation for this may be the same as for involuntary redundancy. The difference is that the business may not force anyone to leave; instead they may offer redundancy packages to those who wish to take them. This could be an attractive proposition for someone who (a) is close to retirement or (b) has another job already lined up.
Retirement	The situation where an employee has decided that they are at the end of their working life. Note that there is not a mandatory retirement age in Australia.
Dismissal	The situation in which an employee is fired. This only occurs in extreme situations, as employers in large businesses can be faced with prosecution for unfair dismissal if they fire someone without just cause. There is usually a process that must be followed to dismiss an employee. This will be stated in the agreement if the business has one.

TABLE 2.5 Types of termination

2.5.3 Entitlement considerations

Entitlements are the things that are owed to employees. Full-time and part-time workers are entitled to get their holiday and long service leave paid out when their employment is terminated. It is not usual for sick leave to be paid out, although some businesses do this.

Redundancy payments would be required if the business found itself in a situation where some or all employees were to be made redundant.

Managers would need to consider the costs of paying out the entitlements of employees. In the case of redundancies, this could be very costly. It is not unusual for a business to insist that employees do not save too much annual leave so that there is not a huge payment when the employee resigns. The details of what the employee is entitled to will be stated in the relevant **award** or **agreement**.

2.5.4 Transition considerations

Transition is the process of moving from one position to another. Some employers assist employees when they leave a business and go through a period of transition to the next job or to retirement. Together with senior management, human resource managers would look at **transition considerations** and decide whether or not to assist employees as they transition to new employment. Note that employees are not obliged to accept any assistance offered.

At Holden, for example, the closure of the manufacturing arm of the business in Australia resulted in many hundreds of redundancies in Victoria and South Australia. The human resource manager offered workers, who were soon to be made redundant, training courses in résumé writing, using LinkedIn to search for new positions or post their profiles in the hope of attracting potential new employers, and writing job applications. As many employees had limited experience or skills outside of manufacturing, these offers were welcomed by employees, keeping them motivated in their final years at Holden. Most workplaces will also provide a reference for employees who resign or are made redundant, but there is no obligation to do this.

> **Hint**
> A quick internet search will provide you with several examples of current redundancy situations in Australian businesses. Try to find at least one current example (within 4 years), taking note of the reason that the redundancy situation occurred, the way in which the employees were notified and, if possible, the details of what the redundant employees actually received.

2.6   Workplace relations

2.6.1 Workplace relations overview

Workplace relations refers to the ways in which wages and conditions of work are determined in workplaces.

Australia's national workplace relations system

The current system (correct in 2022) that determines workplace relations was established by the *Fair Work Act 2009* (Cwlth). There have been several amendments to the original legislation.

> **Australia's workplace relations laws**
> As set out in the Fair Work Act and other workplace legislation, the key elements of our workplace relations framework are:
> - a safety net of minimum terms and conditions of employment
> - a system of enterprise-level collective bargaining underpinned by bargaining obligations and rules governing industrial action
> - provision for individual flexibility arrangements as a way to allow an individual worker and an employer to make flexible work arrangements that meet their genuine needs, provided that the employee is better off overall
> - protections against unfair or unlawful termination of employment
> - protection of the freedom of both employers and employees to choose whether or not to be represented by a third party in workplace matters and the provision of rules governing the rights and responsibilities of employer and employee representatives.
>
> Australia's workplace relations laws are enacted by the Commonwealth Parliament. The practical application of the Fair Work Act in workplaces is overseen by the Fair Work Commission and the Fair Work Ombudsman.
>
> From Attorney-General's Department. (2022) Australia's national workplace relations system. Australian Government.
> https://www.ag.gov.au/industrial-relations/australias-national-workplace-relations-system

2.6.2 Participants in the workplace

There are quite a few stakeholders in the process of determining wages and conditions of work. The extent to which they are involved differs according to the size of the business, the nature of the industry in which the business operates and whether the jobs involved require scarce skills.

Human resource managers

Human resource managers are involved in workplace relations in a number of ways, but of course smaller businesses would not have specific managers to deal with this. It may just form part of a manager or owner's general role in the business. There are three stages at which the human resource manager might be involved in workplace relations.

1   Human resource managers are often involved as employer representatives in the process of negotiating new agreements. This can involve long discussions with workers and/or their unions, keeping in mind the legal requirements as well as the business's financial situation.

2   Human resource managers are responsible for making sure that the agreements are implemented correctly. New levels of wages may need to be organised and the details of new leave arrangements or other work conditions will have to be systematically introduced. The timing of implementation will have to be carefully planned so that workers receive all their entitlements on the correct dates. Control is essential, as the correct amounts of money must be paid and the workers must abide by all leave arrangements and other conditions of work.

3   Human resource managers may be required to negotiate in times of industrial unrest and disputes. If previous negotiations regarding enterprise agreements have failed and industrial action (such as a strike) has resulted, then the human resource manager may need to plan a new strategy and implement some control measures so that no harm is done to the business. They may also have to prepare the information required by the Fair Work Commission if the matter ends up being taken to this institution.

Employees

Employees are involved as it is their wages and conditions of work that are at stake in this process. Employees need to ensure that they are satisfied with the way in which the employer pays them and provides the agreed conditions, and may take industrial action if they are not.

Unions

Unions are bodies that represent groups of employees. Traditionally unions were organised according to trades (hence the term 'trade unions'), but today they represent a wide range of professions as well as trades. They exist to ensure that workers' rights are protected.

Examples include the Australian Education Union (AEU), Transport Workers' Union (TWU) and Australian Workers' Union (AWU). The Australian Council of Trade Unions (ACTU) is the peak union body that represents the interests of working Australians at a national level. This means that it is the organisation that represents all other unions when talks may be required; for example, with the federal government.

Employer associations

Employer associations are bodies that represent employer groups. They are a bit like unions for businesses. They provide advice and support for businesses and may lobby the government over matters that concern them. Examples of employer associations include the Australian Medical Association (AMA, which represents doctors), the Master Builders Australia (MB), CPA Australia (which represents chartered practising accountants), the Australian Industry Group and the Victorian Chamber of Commerce and Industry (VCCI).

The Fair Work Commission

The **Fair Work Commission** is the national workplace relations tribunal that is independent from the government of the day. It has the power to establish the safety net of minimum workplace conditions, oversee enterprise bargaining, monitor and approve industrial action, resolve disputes through mediation and arbitration, and monitor termination of employment.

2.6.3 Awards and agreements

Business owners and/or managers need to decide if they are going to offer their employees the minimum legal wages and conditions (modern awards), or whether they are prepared to offer more and/or different wages and conditions to better suit their situation.

Awards

We have a 'safety net' in Australia that comprises the National Employment Standards (NES), which apply to all employees, and the modern awards that state the minimum pay rates and conditions of work that apply to specific industries. It is illegal to pay workers less than the award wages. Awards are determined by the Fair Work Commission.

Awards are less expensive for businesses, but as they provide low levels of wages, businesses risk not attracting highly skilled employees. The minimum wage is reviewed every year by the Fair Work Commission after hearing submissions from unions and employer associations. Following the election of the Albanese-lead Labor Government in May 2022, the government made a submission to the Fair Work Commission to encourage an increase in the minimum wage to meet the increase in inflation, which was 5.1% at the time.

Agreements

Enterprise agreements are made collectively at workplaces. They state the pay and conditions of work for all employees with the one employer. This does not mean that all employees receive the same pay rates. There would be tables for each occupation and level of skill and/or qualification that show pay levels across the life of the agreement. Usually an agreement lasts for 3 to 5 years. New agreements must be approved by the Fair Work Commission and one of the factors that is considered is that the employees must be 'better off overall' than if they were just provided with the award pay and conditions.

The main benefit of offering agreements is that they can be structured to suit the needs of both the employer and the employee. If done well, there may be pay increases linked to productivity increases. There can be flexible work practices included. As the pay rates are higher than award rates, they can attract highly skilled employees to a workplace.

The difficulties are that they can be time-consuming to negotiate (or bargain), and if there are vastly different positions, it may result in some form of industrial action such as stop-work meetings, strikes, work-to-rule, go slows or boycotts. If this happens during the period of negotiating a new agreement, and the required notice is given, then it may be considered by the Fair Work Commission to be 'protected action', and workers cannot be dismissed for being involved. They will, however, have their wages docked if they go on strike for the period of time that they are not working.

Any type of industrial action is taken only as a last resort, after discussions and negotiations have failed to make the impact that the workers feel is necessary. If this action still fails and the workers and employer cannot come to an agreement, a **dispute resolution** process may be required.

2.6.4 Dispute resolution process

If the employer and employees find that there is a dispute about pay or conditions of work, there needs to be a clear process that is followed to resolve it. It is in nobody's interests to have the dispute linger over months or years. Think back to the dispute that the paramedics had with the Victorian Government. It took a couple of years to resolve.

Grievance procedures state the steps that should be followed when a person has a grievance (complaint or concern). These are specifically written for individual workplaces. The documentation required and the people to whom the grievance should be reported will be stated. The process would normally involve some sort of **mediation** (i.e. the involvement of a third party to help resolve the issue) or **conciliation** (where a third party makes suggestions that could break the impasse).

In the case of workplace relations, sometimes matters cannot be resolved at the workplace. The ultimate stage in the process is **arbitration**, where the Fair Work Commission makes a legally binding decision to resolve the situation.

The Fair Work Ombudsman provides a great deal of assistance to both employers and employees, and outlines the procedures below.

Legal requirements under the Fair Work Act

Employees have access to the dispute resolution procedure set out in the award or agreement that covers them. This procedure can be used to settle disputes related to that award or agreement, or to the National Employment Standards.

Awards

Dispute resolution clauses can vary between awards, but generally have a similar approach to resolution procedures, including:

1 Resolution within the workplace

The employee and their manager must first try to resolve the dispute through discussion. If this is unsuccessful, then senior management discusses the matter with the employee to try and resolve the dispute. This could involve one or more escalations to senior managers, depending on the structure of the business.

2 Resolution outside the workplace

An employee, the employer or their representatives may refer the dispute to the Fair Work Commission after all appropriate steps have been taken within the workplace. The Fair Work Commission can deal with a dispute through conciliation, mediation or, if agreed by the parties, arbitration.

If the dispute still isn't resolved, the Fair Work Commission can use any method of dispute resolution permitted by the Fair Work Act that it considers appropriate to ensure the dispute is settled.

Enterprise agreements

The parties to an enterprise agreement agree to a dispute resolution procedure during the bargaining process. Before approving an enterprise agreement, the Fair Work Commission must check that it contains a dispute resolution clause which:

- has a procedure that requires or allows the Fair Work Commission or another independent person to settle disputes about any matters arising under the agreement or the NES

- allows employees to have a representative.

The Fair Work Regulations provide a model dispute resolution term that can be included in enterprise agreements. Check your award or agreement to see what dispute resolution process applies to your workplace. Visit www.fairwork.gov.au/employment-conditions/awards.

For more information on how the Fair Work Commission can assist with disputes at work see www.fairwork.gov.au/tools-and-resources/best-practice-guides/effective-dispute-resolution.

Hint

There are clearly opposing points of view in every workplace relations dispute. Keep this in mind when reading questions on this topic. As a student of this subject, you are probably required to answer in the best interests of the business, which may sometimes, but not always, conflict with the demands of the employees and their unions. If you can propose a win–win situation, then the dispute time will be minimised and all parties will benefit.

Because there are political considerations, it is not unusual for changes to be made to legislation that affect workplace relations. There are many websites that you can access to ensure that you are absolutely up to date with this topic:

- the Fair Work Ombudsman for a Factsheet on the dispute resolution process
- Australian Unions to learn more about how unions operate and to find more examples
- VCCI to learn more about the different services that it provides to Victorian businesses
- the Fair Work Commission to access information on different awards; check the ones relevant to your part-time job to see if you are being paid correctly!

Glossary

agreements Documents that state the pay and conditions of work for groups of employees with the same employer.

arbitration The process of making a binding decision to resolve a dispute.

awards Industry-specific documents that outline the minimum wages and conditions for occupations.

business objectives Goals that the owners and/or managers of a business hope to achieve.

career advancement The process to gaining promotion or a better position in one's chosen field.

conciliation The process of getting an objective third party to make suggestions about possible solutions to assist two parties to resolve a dispute.

dismissal The situation in which an employee is fired.

dispute resolution The process of finding a solution to a disagreement about wages and conditions of work.

employee observation A method of performance management whereby an employee is watched and evaluated doing their job. It can be performed by managers and/or peers.

employer associations Bodies that represent employer groups and protect their interests.

entitlements Financial or other considerations that are owed to an employee.

Fair Work Commission The independent national workplace relations tribunal.

Four Drive Theory Lawrence and Nohria's theory based on a belief that all people have four major drives that need to be satisfied in order to be motivated: the drive to acquire, the drive to bond, the drive to learn and the drive to defend.

Goal Setting Theory Locke and Latham's theory is based on the belief that by setting goals that are both specific and challenging, followed by constructive feedback, an employee is more likely to be motivated by satisfaction at the sense of achievement and completion of tasks.

grievance procedures The steps that should be followed when a person has a complaint or concern.

human resource management (HRM) The management of workplace tasks that relate to the employment, retention and termination of employees.

human resources The employees of a business.

management by objectives (MBO) A process of managers and employees defining and agreeing on objectives that are to be achieved.

Maslow's Hierarchy of Needs A belief that people progress through five stages of needs as they mature and develop, moving to the next stage only when the previous one has been satisfied.

mediation The process of getting an objective third party to try to assist two parties to resolve a dispute.

motivation The practices or factors that drive a person to perform at their best.

motivation strategies Practices or options that can be implemented to try to motivate workers.

off-the-job training The development of skills that occurs away from the workplace, often involving courses.

on-the-job training The development of skills that occurs at the workplace, usually during normal working hours.

performance appraisal An evaluation of an employee's work over a set period of time.

performance management Implementing strategies to achieve maximum effort and application from employees.

performance-related pay A situation where the salary that is earned is related to work targets.

redundancy The situation in which there is no longer a position for one or more employees at an organisation.

resignation The situation where an employee chooses to leave a workplace, but is not yet retiring.

retirement The situation in which a person ends their working life.

sanctions Penalties for undesirable behaviour.

self-evaluation An assessment of the employee's performance at work conducted by themselves.

9780170465137

strategies Practices or actions implemented with the aim of achieving a particular effect.

support Assistance to help an employee to perform better.

termination The point at which an employee leaves an organisation.

training A process aimed at improving technical skill levels.

transition considerations Strategies that businesses may put in place to assist workers as they transit or move to new employment.

unions Organisations that represent the interests of groups of workers (usually based on similar occupations).

workplace relations The ways in which wages and conditions of work are determined in workplaces.

CHAPTER 2 – GLOSSARY

Revision summary

The first column in the table below has the key knowledge points of Unit 3 Area of Study 2. Read the suggestions in the second column for ways that you can complete notes that will be useful for preparation for both School-assessed Coursework tasks as well as your end-of-year exam.

Unit 3 Area of Study 2 Human resource management	Suggestions for summary notes
The relationship between human resource management and business objectives	Write one sentence to describe this relationship, then provide three examples of human resources practices that can lead to the achievement of three different business objectives.
Key principles of the following theories of motivation: • Hierarchy of Needs (Maslow)	• Explain what a needs-based theory is. • Draw Maslow's pyramid. • Briefly explain how Maslow's theory could be applied to a workplace (all five levels of need).
• Goal Setting Theory (Locke and Latham)	• Explain how a goal-setting theory works. • Describe Locke and Latham's theory. • Define the term 'moderator variables' and explain how three of them can affect the goal-setting process. • Explain how a human resource manager could use this theory in a business today.
• the Four Drive Theory (Lawrence and Nohria)	• Explain what a contingency theory is. • Outline the four drives. • Explain how managers could use this theory in a business today.
Motivation strategies including performance-related pay, career advancement, investment in training, support strategies and sanction strategies	List each of these strategies and write one advantage and one disadvantage for each as well as well as whether it would work better in the short term or long term (use the table from page 27 of *A+ VCE Business Management Study Notes* to assist here).
Advantages and disadvantages of motivation strategies and their effect on short- and long-term employee motivation	
Training options including on-the-job and off-the-job training, and the advantages and disadvantages of each	Define each term, provide two examples of each and one advantage and one disadvantage of each term.
Performance management strategies to achieve both business and employee objectives, including management by objectives, appraisals, self-evaluation and employee observation	Define each term and list one business and one employee objective that each one could help to achieve.
Termination management including retirement, redundancy, resignation and dismissal, entitlement considerations and transition considerations	Define the four types of termination. Write next to each whether the termination type is decided by the employer or the employee. Outline what is meant by entitlements and list two entitlement considerations. Outline what transition means in this context and what some transition considerations could be.

›› The roles of participants in the workplace including human resource managers, employees, employer associations, unions and the Fair Work Commission	Briefly outline the roles of these groups. List at least two examples of unions and employer associations as well. Make sure you link it to a workplace – pay, conditions of work who they assist/represent etc. (Yes, I can hear you thinking 'it won't be brief if I add all of that in'.)
Awards and agreements as methods of determining wages and conditions of work	Write definitions of both terms as well as the advantages and disadvantages of both from the employers' and employees' points of view.
An overview of the dispute resolution process including mediation and arbitration	Finally, define the three terms and write out the steps that are involved in a dispute resolution process.

VCE Business Management Study Design 2023–2027 p. 18, © VCAA 2022

CHAPTER 2 – REVISION SUMMARY

Exam practice

Solutions for this section start on page 100.

Question 1 (1 mark) ⬤◯◯

Describe one benefit for a business having motivated employees.

Question 2 (2 marks) ⬤◯◯

Why is Maslow's theory called a 'hierarchy of needs'?

Question 3 (4 marks) ⬤⬤◯

Explain why Locke and Latham said that goals need to be both specific and challenging in order to raise motivation levels.

Question 4 (2 + 2 + 2 + 2 = 8 marks) ⬤⬤⬤

List the four drives as stated by Lawrence and Nohria, with one example for each showing how they can be applied in a business.

Question 5 (4 marks) ⬤⬤◯

Explain one advantage and one disadvantage of using performance-related pay to motivate employees.

Question 6 (2 marks) ⬤◯◯

Distinguish between on-the-job and off-the-job training.

Question 7 (2 marks) ⬤◯◯

List two advantages of on-the-job training and two advantages of off-the-job training.

Question 8 (2 marks) ⬤◯◯

Explain why businesses conduct performance appraisals.

Question 9 (2 marks) ⬤◯◯

List two performance management strategies besides appraisals.

Question 10 (4 marks) ⬤⬤◯

Compare redundancies with resignation as forms of termination of employment.

Question 11 (4 marks) ⬤⬤◯

Compare the roles of unions and employer associations.

Question 12 (2 marks) ⬤⬤◯

Outline one strength and one weakness for a business of offering employees award pay and conditions.

Question 13 (2 marks) ⬤⬤⬤

Distinguish between mediation and arbitration as methods of dispute resolution.

Question 14 (2 marks) ⬤⬤◯

Under what conditions can industrial action be deemed 'protected action'?

Question 15 (1 mark) ⬤◯◯

Outline one way human resource managers could be involved in workplace relations.

CHAPTER 2 – EXAM PRACTICE

Question 16 (4 marks) ©VCAA 2017 SA Q3b ●●

Car Bright is a car cleaning and detailing service business owned by Aaron Bright. It charges higher prices than its competitors. Following a staff survey, it was found that some of Car Bright's employees are lacking motivation. In addition, some customers have complained of slow service and that their cars have been returned not fully cleaned.

Aaron is considering investing in training for his employees. Discuss a suitable training option that could be used for Car Bright's employees.

Question 17 (3 marks) ©VCAA 2017 SA Q2 ●●●

Distinguish between mediation and arbitration as a means of dispute resolution.

Question 18 (6 marks) ©VCAA 2018 SA Q1c ●●●

123 Childcare Centre is a business operating as a partnership. It provides childcare services for children aged five and under. Mary Kidd, one of the partners at the centre, wants to meet the demand for high-quality and reliable childcare in her local area. However, employees complain of long hours and their motivation is low. Staff turnover is a problem and Mary is unsure of how to address this.

Maslow's Hierarchy of Needs has been suggested to Mary as an appropriate motivational theory for improving employee performance. Describe this theory of motivation and explain how it could be applied at 123 Childcare Centre to reduce the level of staff turnover.

Question 19 (6 marks) ©VCAA 2019 SA Q6 ●●●

With reference to a contemporary business case study, explain how managers could apply **one** theory of motivation and a related motivational strategy to successfully manage employees.

Question 20 (10 marks) ©VCAA 2020 SA Q4 ●●

When motivating employees, managers can use a range of strategies. Evaluate **two** different motivation strategies. Identify and justify which one of these strategies would be most effective for the short-term motivation of employees and which one would be most effective for the long-term motivation of employees.

Exam practice: Case study A

Solutions for this section start on page 103.

Solutions for this section start on page 103.

CASE STUDY A	DStore is a chain of large stores similar to Kmart and Big W. Its head office, where the buyers, finance and logistics staff are located, is in Melbourne. Recently 15 staff members from the finance department won lots of money in TattsLotto. Many of the winners had worked at DStore for more than 15 years and they have now all tendered their resignations with 2 weeks' notice. They all worked in the accounts department, paying suppliers and managing payroll for staff. Betty Bottle is the human resource manager. Her first step is to ensure that the exiting employees get their entitlements.

Questions

Question 1 (1 mark)

Define resignation.

Question 2 (2 marks)

Outline two entitlements that will need to be provided to the staff who are resigning.

Question 3 (4 marks)

Fifteen new employees need to be hired to replace those who resigned. Betty has been in discussion with senior management about the high cost of employees' wages. The finance manager has suggested that rather than use an enterprise agreement, DStore could just offer the award wages and conditions to the new employees. Discuss whether this would be a good decision for DStore.

Question 4 (4 marks)

Some of the new employees who were hired to replace those who left are not familiar with the specific accounting software that DStore uses. Compare the similarities and differences of providing the required training at DStore through on-the-job or off-the-job methods.

> The new employees have been at DStore for a year now. They are concerned because they often have to work overtime, but never get paid any extra. They are considering taking industrial action if there is not a solution.

Question 5 (6 marks)

Explain three steps in the process of dispute resolution, including the role of a different participant in each step of the process.

Question 6 (3 marks)

Identify and explain a performance management strategy that would be appropriate for the new employees after 1 year at DStore.

Total = 20 marks

Exam practice: Case study B

Solutions for this section start on page 104.

> Shako is a large company that operates a chain of retail clothing stores. There are Shako stores in all capital cities throughout Australia and New Zealand. The company employs a large number of casual employees who are studying at university and have no plans for a career in retail. They consider the job to be simply a source of income to get them through university. Eileen Emerald is the human resource manager at Shako. Senior management have given her the task to lift the motivation, and hence productivity rates, of both the full-time and casual employees.

CASE STUDY B

Questions

Question 1 (2 marks) ⬤◯◯

Outline the relationship between human resource management and business objectives.

Question 2 (4 marks) ⬤⬤⬤

Outline Maslow's theory of motivation and explain how it could be used to motivate the full-time employees of Shako.

Question 3 (8 marks) ⬤⬤⬤

Compare Locke and Latham's Goal Setting Theory and Lawrence and Nohria's Four Drive Theory and evaluate which would be more effective in motivating the casual employees at Shako.

Question 4 (3 + 3 = 6 marks) ⬤⬤⬤

Discuss the advantages and disadvantages in both the short and long term of using:

a career advancement as a motivation strategy for full-time employees

b performance-related pay as a motivation strategy for casual employees.

Total = 20 marks

Chapter 3
Area of Study 3: Operations management

Area of Study summary

The emphasis of this area of study is the production of goods and/or services. Again, the way that this is managed will determine if the business's objectives (see Chapter 1) are achieved.

You will need an understanding of the inputs, processes and outputs (key elements of operations) that relate to both a manufacturer and a service provider. You will need real examples of both of these. Keep in mind that some businesses provide both goods and services.

Most of this area of study relates to the strategies that are available to the operations manager to achieve their business objectives. These strategies could be related to technology or quality, or they may be related to three separate strategies that involve the efficient use of materials: materials management, lean production and the minimisation of waste. It is very important that you answer any questions that relate to this topic clearly to distinguish between these three.

Finally, there are two concepts that the operations manager must consider: corporate social responsibility and global options for both inputs and processes.

Area of Study 3 Outcome 3

On completing this outcome, you should be able to:

- analyse the relationship between business objectives and **operations management**
- propose and evaluate strategies to improve the **efficiency** and **effectiveness** of business operations.

The key skills demonstrated in this outcome are:

- identify, define, describe and apply business management concepts and terms
- interpret, discuss, compare and evaluate business information, theories and ideas
- analyse case studies and contemporary examples of management
- apply business management knowledge to practical and/or simulated business situations
- propose, justify and evaluate management strategies to improve business performance.

VCE Business Management Study Design 2023–2027 p. 19, © VCAA 2022

3.1   Operations management overview

3.1.1 Operations management and business objectives

Operations management refers to the task of managing the process that transforms resources into finished goods and/or services.

Relationship to business objectives

Most businesses exist to generate profit, which goes to the owners or is distributed to shareholders. An organisation that effectively manages its production of goods and/or services through wise implementation of operations management **strategies** will use resources efficiently and keep customers satisfied, resulting in increased profit levels. Generally, an operations manager would be aiming to increase productivity (i.e. the amount of output per set of inputs per period of time), so that the organisation can become more competitive. Competitiveness refers to an organisation's ability to match or better its rivals in a given market. If the operations are being managed efficiently, then costs will be minimised, the quality of the product should increase and delivery times and accuracy should improve. All these aspects can really give one business the edge over the others in its market.

3.1.2 Key elements of operations of manufacturers and service providers

All operations systems take inputs and process them to make outputs. These three **key elements of operations** are essential when considering operations management (see Table 3.1).

1   **Inputs** are the resources that are necessary to make the product. They may include:

- natural resources (raw materials such as wheat, cotton or water)
- capital (machinery, information technology systems, electricity, money, trucks, factories)
- labour (workers, managers and their skills and knowledge).

> **Hint**
> Keep the categories of resources (inputs) in mind as they will appear again in Unit 4 Area of Study 2 when the redeployment of resources is looked at as a change strategy.

Sometimes the information that is available can also be considered an input.

2   **Processes** refer to the actions performed on the inputs to transform them into the finished product. Processes may include baking, cutting, transporting, filing and cleaning.

> **Hint**
> One way to ensure that you are writing about processes correctly is to ensure that you use verbs. An easy way to do this and keep on track is to try to use words that end in 'ing'. Inputs and outputs tend to be nouns.

3   **Outputs** refer to the finished products. These can be goods or services. **Goods** are tangible, can be stored for later use and often the consumption occurs separately from the purchase. Examples of goods are cars, biscuits, carpet and books. **Services**, on the other hand, are intangible, they cannot be stored and the consumption usually occurs with the purchase, meaning that the consumer is involved directly. Examples of services include haircuts, gardening, transport and medical procedures. While the fundamental aspects of operations management remain the same, they will differ in minor ways according to the type and size of businesses. The differences will be particularly noticeable in firms that provide goods compared with those that provide services. This may be apparent in Table 3.1.

Type of business	Inputs	Processes	Outputs
Cleaning business (service provider)	Detergents, buckets, dusters, mops, vacuum cleaners	Washing windows, vacuuming floors, cleaning toilets and washbasins	A cleaned office and house
Bus company (service provider)	Buses, mechanics, drivers, administrative staff, tools, tickets, sheds/garages, petrol bowsers	Transporting children to school, booking tours, maintaining buses, negotiating contracts	Tours, transportation of school children, transportation of local residents
Clothing manufacturer (goods provider)	Fabric, thread, zips, sewing machines, cutting machines, design programs for computers, machinists, designers, administrative staff, warehouse workers, electricity, factory	Designing clothes, cutting and sewing fabric, pressing, stacking, ordering materials, selling, invoicing, delivering clothes to retailers	The range of clothing that has been produced
Bakery (goods provider)	Wheat, sugar, fruit, yeast, milk, water, factory, trucks, bakers, ovens, mixing machines, drivers, electricity	Mixing and baking the ingredients, packaging, ordering supplies, transporting bread to customers, invoicing customers	Bread, cakes, pies and other baked goods

TABLE 3.1 Examples of the key elements of operations for goods and services providers

3.1.3 Corporate social responsibility and operations

While business managers and owners may know how to maximise their production using the strategies outlined in Section 3.2, there are several factors that they need to consider. These include corporate social responsibility considerations. **Corporate social responsibility (CSR)** is where businesses take responsibility for their actions that affect the wider community through the use of ethical practices.

Environmental sustainability of inputs

An important consideration for many businesses is **environmental sustainability**; that is, whether the resources that are used in production are from a sustainable source. Timber is a good example of this. Furniture is often advertised as being made from plantations that are not old-growth forests or scarce timbers such as Huon pine. Restaurants can look up the Sustainable Seafood Guide, which is produced by the Australian Marine Conservation Society, to ensure that the fish and other seafood products they purchase and cook are not from endangered species.

Amount of waste generated from processes

The methods used to transform the inputs into the finished goods and services should be such that they do not cause pollution. If there is unavoidable **waste**, it might be able to be put to use in some way in the community. Planet Ark assists businesses by taking waste products and recycling them. Recycled paper is a good example of this.

Production of outputs

The goods and services that are produced should not cause problems for society – they should enhance the quality of our lives. While there are laws that prevent the production of some socially undesirable products, the managers of a business that is demonstrating corporate social responsibility will ensure that it goes beyond this. More than 900 businesses are signatories to the

Australian Packaging Covenant (APC). This is a scheme where government, industry and community groups agree to look for solutions to design more-sustainable packaging. This also includes methods of reducing the amount of packaging used and reducing waste. With the increase of online shopping, businesses that want to show their corporate social responsibility credentials would consider the packaging very carefully.

3.2 Operations management strategies

Section 3.1 explained what operations management means and how it can assist in achieving a **business's objectives**. But what if the system is evaluated and is found to be lacking in some areas? Perhaps the productivity levels are not where they should be; perhaps customers have been taking their business elsewhere. In cases such as these, the operations manager would need to try to determine the causes of the problems, then implement a strategy that might improve the degree of success.

Within each strategy area, there are a number of options that the operations manager may decide to select to optimise operations. It is probable that they would choose a combination of strategies, depending on the areas that they wish to address. There are two overarching aims for businesses. These are to improve their **efficiency** (making the best possible use of resources) and **effectiveness** (achieving stated goals and objectives). The following strategies can assist businesses to improve both.

> **Hint**
>
> Don't forget that the Business Management Study Design lists the strategies that you need to learn. This means that you could get specific questions on each of them. Don't make the mistake of thinking that you only need to know one quality strategy, one materials management strategy and so on.

3.2.1 Technological developments

Use of technological developments

One of the best ways to improve productivity levels is to increase efficiency through the implementation of **technology**. Technological developments can help the operations manager in a number of ways.

- More may be able to be produced.
- The quality may be enhanced.
- Fewer errors may be made.
- Less waste may result.

Problems associated with the implementation of technology

While technology can provide some great advantages for businesses, there are also problems that the operations manager would need to consider before implementing new or updated technology:

- Cost: Technology is expensive, and it is often out-of-date almost as soon as it has been purchased! Keeping up with the latest technology can be a very expensive exercise.
- Training: It's all very well to have the latest technology, but if the employees don't know how to make the most of it, it can be a waste. Some or all employees would probably have to be trained in the use and repair of the new technology for its implementation to really be effective.
- Repairs: In some cases, staff will need to be employed to maintain and repair the new technology, whether it involves the use of advanced computer programs or manufacturing machinery. This is an added expense for the business.
- Redundancies: Technology can sometimes replace workers. Machines may do the work that was previously performed by people (e.g. self-serve checkouts in supermarkets) or may simply do the work more quickly, leading to fewer workers being required to maintain productivity levels.

Technologies and their different uses

Technology improvements can assist in the production of both goods and services. Indeed, the use of computers and related information and communications technology in the service sector is vital.

There are many different types of technology that an operations manager may look at implementing, and they will vary according to the type of organisation. Some technologies can assist in materials management, such as security and stocktake systems.

Sometimes businesses may implement new technology that is not directly related to production. For example, motels install chargers for electric vehicles with the goal of attracting travellers who would like to take advantage of the convenience of this.

Here is a list of technologies that are useful for the actual production of goods and services.

Automated production lines

Many goods are made on **production lines**. When these are automated (i.e. mechanised, resulting in less human intervention) the speed of the process, and often the accuracy, increases. Many food and drink items are produced on **automated production lines**.

Robotics

Robots are machines that have been created to perform tasks that are usually done by people. They have been used in manufacturing for many years doing jobs that are dangerous or repetitive; however, there are many other uses as well. Here are some business examples.

- Car manufacturers use **robotics** for assembly and to spray-paint cars so that people do not breathe in the paint fumes.
- Robots are used in mines to test air quality to determine if it is safe for the human workers.
- There is increasing application for robots in medical settings where a high degree of precision is required for some operations. In 2020, the Royal Adelaide Hospital introduced robots to deliver clean sheets, meals, pharmacy items and waste to free up nurses so they can concentrate on caring for patients.
- Robots can also be used in situations which are not hazardous or do not require precision. Dodee Paidang is a Thai restaurant in Melbourne that uses a robot named Bellabot as a waiter. This is cost effective for the business, especially when there are staff shortages.

> **Hint**
> Learn more about robotics at:
> - https://data61.csiro.au/en/Our-Research/Our-Work/Robotics-Family
> - https://www.foodanddrinkbusiness.com.au/news/robotics-in-a-connected-world
> - https://robycstechnology.com.au/robotic-technology-australia/
> - https://www.incremental.com.au/blog/robotics-move-into-businesses/
> - https://www.theage.com.au/national/victoria/robot-waiters-are-here-so-who-gets-the-tips-and-what-if-the-service-is-slow-20211118-p59a19.html.

Computer-aided design

Using computers to design, rather than drafting by hand, means that designers can easily experiment with variations of design with less effort and time. **Computer-aided design (CAD)** can also assist in maximising the use of resources (inputs) by minimising any potential wastage.

Computer-aided manufacturing

Computer programs can often run machines, telling them what the production run should consist of in terms of time, number of units, sizes and so on. They can be changed easily when required. **Computer-aided manufacturing (CAM)** can assist with minimising faults and improving quality.

Artificial intelligence

Artificial intelligence (AI) is considered to be extremely valuable to Australia and its economy, to the point where the federal government is investing heavily in it.

The CSIRO, in its AI Roadmap, defines and explains AI as:

> A collection of interrelated technologies used to solve problems autonomously and perform tasks to achieve defined objectives, in some cases without explicit guidance from a human being. Subfields of AI include machine learning, computer vision, human language technologies, robotics, knowledge representation and other scientific fields. The power of AI comes from a convergence of technologies. AI is a general-purpose technology that can be used to increase the efficiency, safety and quality of production processes in almost every industry. AI is already being used to solve challenging problems in health, welfare, safety, environment, energy, infrastructure, transport, education and other sectors.

Source: Hajkowicz SA, Karimi S, Wark T, et al. (2019) Artificial intelligence: Solving problems, growing the economy and improving our quality of life. CSIRO Data61, Australia. https://data61.csiro.au/en/Our-Research/Our-Work/AI-Roadmap

---

The AI Roadmap provides many examples of current AI use including the following.

- An on-farm agricultural robot Agbot II developed by the Queensland University of Technology could save Australia's farm sector AU$1.3 billion per year by automating weed removal and improving agricultural productivity.

- Mining operations in the Pilbara region of Western Australia are among the world's most automated. Fortescue operates 112 driverless trucks with a 30% productivity gain. BHP has 50 autonomous trucks at its Jimblebar site and 20 autonomous drills statewide. Launched in 2008 Rio Tinto's mine-of-the-future has 140 automated trucks, over 11 automated drills, and 60% of train kilometres are in autonomous mode.

- An AI system for detecting skin cancer (which could become a smartphone app) performed 'on par' with 21 certified dermatologists. In Australia 13 280 new cases of melanoma were diagnosed in 2016 and 1770 people died from the disease. Earlier diagnosis enabled by AI will save lives.

Source: Hajkowicz SA, Karimi S, Wark T, et al. (2019) Artificial intelligence: Solving problems, growing the economy and improving our quality of life. CSIRO Data61, Australia. https://data61.csiro.au/en/Our-Research/Our-Work/AI-Roadmap

---

Hint

See the following websites for more information about AI.
- https://www.businessaustralia.com/how-we-help/be-more-efficient/work-smarter/can-your-business-benefit-from-ai-
- https://www.industry.gov.au/policies-and-initiatives/artificial-intelligence
- https://digitaleconomy.pmc.gov.au/fact-sheets/artificial-intelligence

Online services

Online services include the development of a website, online ordering and purchasing software. Many businesses cannot operate effectively without a website or the use of an app. This technology is essential for the effective running of the business. It can save time to inform customers of changes via a website, hence increasing the efficiency of its operations.

During the COVID-19 pandemic, businesses relied more than ever on providing online services and not just selling goods. For example, many gyms offered online sessions when lockdowns prevented gyms from opening.

3.2.2 Materials management

Materials are the stock that is used for the production process. They are also sometimes called 'inventory'. The terms materials, stock and inventory tend to be used interchangeably. **Materials management** refers to the systems that are implemented to ensure the right materials are available in the right numbers for the right cost when required. The operations manager has a number of responsibilities regarding materials. They must ensure that there is the correct amount, that the materials are on hand when needed and that the materials are not sitting idle (tying up money) if they are not needed immediately. Materials management includes some basic methods such as conducting regular stocktakes and making sure that there is security to prevent theft. As materials are directly connected with resource use, materials management can assist in increasing efficiency in businesses.

Forecasting

Forecasting requires a prediction of the materials that may be needed in the upcoming period. This is often an automated system that bases its forecast on the previous history of production and the materials that were needed. In some cases, items are automatically reordered when a certain point is noted in the system. This system works equally well for both **manufacturers** and **service providers** where the goods or services that are produced remain quite similar in each time period.

Master production schedule

A **master production schedule (MPS)** is a document that shows what the business plans to produce and the plan to produce it within a given time period. It is part of the tactical planning responsibility of the operations manager. The advantage of an MPS is that it can be tailored to reflect a changing production schedule. A large hotel, for example, can factor in how many functions, room guests or conferences it has coming up over the next month, then plan accordingly.

Materials requirement planning

Once the MPS has been completed, the operations manager can then determine the **materials requirement plan (MRP)**. This document outlines all of the materials that will be required to complete the production targets that have been set out in the MPS. In the case of the hotel (see MPS above), they can estimate how much fruit, vegetables, meat, wine and so on they are going to require. They will also know how many staff will be required to work at the functions or clean the rooms.

Just in Time

Just in Time is a specific materials management strategy that is implemented as part of the supply chain. It requires the operations manager to keep just enough materials on hand to get the workplace through the next production period. The belief behind this strategy is that it is a waste to tie up money in resources that may not be used for some time. There is also the possibility that the actual product may be changed or modified, and the materials in stock might never be required. Most large manufacturers work with a version of this strategy – but it does not always work perfectly. There have been a number of cases in recent years where car manufacturers have had to stand down workers and cease production because supplier companies went on strike. The car manufacturers had limited materials on hand because they worked with 'just in time'. In the preceding hotel example, perishable items such food are often ordered 'just in time' so that they don't end up throwing away food that is past its use-by date.

3.2.3 Quality management

Quality is often defined as a standard that meets the needs/wants of the customer. If the customer is not satisfied, then there may be problems in terms of the control of the quality during some stage of the production process. Quality strategies can assist businesses to achieve effectiveness, particularly if their objectives relate to the satisfaction of customers. There are many quality strategies that can be implemented by an operations manager, some of which look at ways to build quality into the process and others that evaluate the quality of the end product.

Quality control

Quality control refers to methods that simply 'check and reject' items that do not conform to the expected standard. There are several ways that this can be done. The first is **quality checks/audits** where the goods or services are checked either when complete or during the production process to see if the product conforms to the required standard. Hotel operations managers might check rooms after the cleaners have finished to see if they are satisfactory. A tinned fruit processing factory, however, may perform batch testing. This requires a random sample to be taken from each 'batch' or production run. They would check to see if the tinned fruit is the correct weight, the fruit looks and tastes right, the tin is not damaged and so on. Batch testing is especially useful for the production of goods. If the quality checks do detect a problem, it may be the case that the whole production run is ruined – and by then it is too late. This is why so many businesses today look at implementing a quality strategy that is designed to improve the quality of the production process.

Quality assurance

Quality assurance systems (QAS) refers to methods of measuring the quality of a product or process against a standard. There are several different QAS used around the world in many diverse industries; for example, in manufacturing and health care. The website for SAI Global has a great deal of information about a range of quality systems. The information below is an example of this.

The 'Five Ticks' StandardsMark™ (see Figure 3.1) is Australia's most recognised certification mark, providing competitive advantage and differentiation to each product carrying this mark. The StandardsMark™ on a product is an independent assurance to the customer that the product has undergone a rigorous audit and testing program. The StandardsMark™ Scheme requires annual audits of the manufacturing site in addition to the product type testing according to the relevant standard.

FIGURE 3.1 The 'Five Ticks' StandardsMark™

The 'five ticks' StandardsMark™ ISO 9001:2015 is a quality assurance method that is recognised around the world. It comprises a system of best practice processes to improve the quality of the good or service. Firms that are certified as ISO 9000 compliant have met the criteria for certification. The latest standard is ISO 9001:2015. (The 9000 series relates to quality, the 14 000 series relates to environmental standards, the 18 000 series relates to occupational health and safety standards, etc.). It involves a generic quality system that can be implemented no matter whether the business produces goods or services.

ISO 9001:2015 is a generic management system. Generic means that it can be applied to any organisation in any sector – public or private. Management system refers to what the organisation does to manage its processes and procedures such as instructions, forms or records. ISO 9001:2015 is concerned with the way an organisation goes about its work (i.e. its processes), not the end product directly. By establishing a system of performing these processes, there is a greater chance of achieving a consistent, high-quality product. ISO 9001:2015 Management System Standards provide the organisation with a model to follow that incorporates the features that experts in the field have agreed upon as representing the state of the art.

The operating principle of ISO's management system standards is Plan, Do, Check and Act. A cleaning firm would be a good example here, whereby they can implement standards that will ensure that quality is built into the process of providing the service of cleaning. Firms often advertise that they are certified for ISO 9001:2015 Quality Management Systems. This means that they have met the criteria for certification and have implemented all the steps necessary for approval as ISO 9001:2015 certified. Regular audits are a necessary feature of ISO 9001:2015, as inspections by both internal and external auditors will ensure that the standards are being implemented properly over a period of time.

Total Quality Management

Total Quality Management (TQM) is one of the most common forms of a quality system, although it is often adapted to suit the organisation. TQM has the following features:

- a belief in continuous improvement
- an emphasis on teamwork and employee participation to solve quality problems
- customer satisfaction as the main aim.

If a biscuit factory is used as an example, then TQM would mean that all employees are given the opportunity to work in teams to come up with ideas on how to continuously improve the aspects of production that they work on. If these workers identify a problem, then they are probably the ones most likely to come up with a solution to rectify it. Often workers are grouped into quality circles to do this. What is important is that TQM suggests that there is always room for improvement. Workers should try to anticipate the needs of the customer. In TQM, the 'customer' refers to the next person in the production line or further down the line, not just the final user of the product. This means that the workers mixing the biscuit dough must try to always improve their mixing so that the bakers are totally satisfied; the bakers must try to improve their baking methods so that the packaging workers are totally satisfied and so on.

3.2.4 Waste minimisation

A **waste minimisation** strategy links most closely with the objective of improving efficiency. By minimising waste, businesses will be making the best possible use of their resources. Many businesses use the concept of reduce, reuse, recycle in order to minimise waste. This is supported by state and federal governments who wish to pursue action in this area. The Victorian State Government has four goals for businesses as part of its circular economy.

> Victoria's transition to a circular economy will be guided by four goals spanning the life cycle of materials (make, use, recycle and manage). Each goal is designed to maximise value and minimise waste.
>
> - Goal 1 – Design to last, repair and recycle.
> - Goal 2 – Use products to create more value.
> - Goal 3 – Recycle more resources.
> - Goal 4 – Reduce harm from waste and pollution.

Source: State of Victoria (Department of Environment, Land, Water and Planning) (2020) Recycling Victoria: A New Economy. State of Victoria. https://www.vic.gov.au/sites/default/files/2020-02/Recycling%20Victoria%20A%20new%20economy.pdf

Individual businesses also pursue the **reduce**, **reuse**, **recycle** process. Coles launched its Together to Zero Waste program in 2022. This encompasses the following actions:

1 reducing food waste

2 soft-plastic recycling

3 reusable bags

4 sustainable packaging

5 recycling labels on Coles Own Brand products.

Soure: Coles Supermarkets Australia Pty Ltd (2022). Together to Zero Waste.
https://www.coles.com.au/about-coles/sustainability/environment/together-to-zero-waste

3.2.5 Lean management

The main aim of many businesses regarding productivity and competitiveness is to be efficient in terms of lean production. **Lean management** refers to the establishment of systems that will eliminate waste and inefficiencies of any kind in the process of making a good or providing a service.

Examples of waste include:

- idle time

- excess time taken to complete tasks

- unused materials

- discarded materials

- defective products

- excessive wait times between production and distribution.

Whenever waste has been minimised, the business is said to be more efficient and is more likely to remain profitable and competitive. Most large manufacturers around the world such as pharmaceutical companies and sporting-goods manufacturers are now embracing lean production methods. As labour costs in many developing countries are much lower than those in Australia, businesses need to utilise lean manufacturing if they want to be able to compete on an international level. Lean principles are also increasingly used in service industries. Banks utilise lean measures to improve their efficiency and minimise their waste levels. The resources may tend to be different from those in manufacturing, but wasted time and defective products can be just as much a problem for them as they are for manufacturers. Many Australian hospitals (both public and private) rely on lean principles to minimise waste. As funding becomes increasingly tight for hospitals, they need to ensure that every resource, especially medical equipment, medicines and staff, is put to use well.

Businesses can ensure that they incorporate lean management methods by implementing four interconnected principles that are sometimes collectively known as the Toyota Way.

- **Pull**: This refers to demand pull, or not producing items until the customer has ordered the product. It will prevent a build-up of unwanted stock being produced.

- **One-piece flow**: This is a system that aims to complete production of one unit at a time in a continuous flow. It is the opposite of batch production.

- **Zero defects**: This is a process of identifying production errors or defects at the stage in which they occur. It prevents them from being passed on to the next stage of production.

- **Takt**: This word means timing in German and refers to the maximum time required to complete production to meet customer demand. One-piece flow relies on the takt being carefully calculated to prevent bottlenecks and/or idle time.

Source: https://www.fourprinciples.com/lean/

3.3   Global considerations

3.3.1 Global sourcing of inputs

It is not unusual for businesses to seek the lowest cost inputs for their production. Often this means purchasing products from other countries. While the cost advantages of this are clear, there can also be problems. For example, an Australian manufacturer that imports berries for their fruit pies from overseas was linked to an outbreak of hepatitis A in 2014. When the Department of Health and Human Services (DHHS) tested their products, there were two that proved to be positive for hepatitis A. Subsequent tests on the products found only one trace amount while other tests were negative. This sort of thing can happen because quality and safety standards in some countries are not as stringent as they are in Australia. Businesses have to weigh up the benefits against the costs, as recalls of products and the damage done to the brand's reputation can be expensive and result in lost market share.

3.3.2 Overseas manufacture

With labour costs in Australia much higher than those in many developing countries, businesses sometimes find it more cost-effective to manufacture overseas. This has been particularly prevalent in the clothing and footwear industry. Blundstone is a good example of this. All of their leather boots are now manufactured in countries such as Vietnam, India and China. They employ their own people at the manufacturing facilities to ensure that the quality of the product is at the standard that their customers expect. Blundstone still manufactures gumboots in Tasmania.

3.3.3 Global outsourcing

Connected with overseas manufacturing is the concept of global **outsourcing**. Sometimes, however, it may be services that are outsourced. In some cases, a business may do both. Call centres for telecommunications and finance businesses are often outsourced to countries such as India and the Philippines. Some large businesses outsource their finance departments to businesses operating in other countries as well.

> **Hint**
>
> To find up-to-date information on this topic, search for the following topics online.
> - Australian Marine Conservation Society's Australia's Sustainable Seafood Guide is useful for restaurants and consumers.
> - Sustainability Victoria has case studies on businesses that have become more environmentally sustainable.
> - Planet Ark has case studies of ways that businesses can reduce their waste from the production process, or at least put it to good use. As they state on their website, 'We work collaboratively and positively with a range of businesses that have a commitment to promoting sustainable resource use, encourage a low carbon lifestyle, and connect people with nature'.
> - The Australian Packaging Covenant website has a complete list of all businesses that are signatories.
> - Austrade provides advice for businesses that are considering operating in a global context.

Glossary

artificial intelligence (AI) The ability of machines to comprehend, act and learn in a similar way to the natural intelligence of humans.

automated production line A series of workstations that are linked technologically to operate with minimal human intervention.

business objectives Goals that the owners and/or managers of a business hope to achieve.

computer-aided design (CAD) Programs that allow designers to create and modify designs for products and processes.

computer-aided manufacturing (CAM) Programs that allow computers to run part or all of the production process.

corporate social responsibility (CSR) Where businesses take responsibility for their actions that impact on the wider community through the use of ethical practices.

effectiveness The process of achieving all stated goals and objectives.

efficiency The process of making the best possible use of resources.

environmental sustainability The process of managing the use of natural resources to ensure that they are not depleted.

forecasting Predicting the materials that may be needed in an upcoming timeframe.

goods Products that are tangible, can be stored for later use and the consumption can occur separately from the purchase.

inputs The resources necessary to make the product.

Just in Time A materials management strategy that is implemented as part of the supply chain whereby just enough materials are kept on hand to get the workplace through the next production period.

key elements of operations The inputs, processes and outputs of a business.

lean management The establishment of systems that will eliminate waste and inefficiencies of any kind in the process of making a good or providing a service.

manufacturers Businesses that produce goods.

master production schedule (MPS) A document that shows what the business plans to produce and the plan to produce it within a given time period.

A+ DIGITAL FLASHCARDS
Revise this topic's key terms and concepts by scanning the QR code or typing the URL into your browser.

https://get.ga/aplus-vce-busmgmt-u34

materials management The systems that are implemented to ensure that the right materials are available in the right numbers for the right cost when required.

materials requirement plan (MRP) A document that outlines all of the materials that will be required to complete the production targets that have been set out in the master production schedule.

one-piece flow An element of lean production that completes production of each item in a continuous fashion.

online services A range of business operations that utilise the internet.

operations management The task of managing the process that transforms resources into finished goods and/or services.

outputs The finished products (either goods or services) that result when inputs have been processed.

outsourcing The process of hiring another business or consultant to complete a task or project.

processes The actions performed on inputs to transform them into finished products.

production line A method of assembling a standardised product by adding components/parts as the product moves along a line.

pull An element of lean production that uses demand to determine the number and types of items produced.

quality A standard that meets the needs and/or wants of the customer.

quality assurance system (QAS) A quality method that involves measuring the quality of a product or process against a standard (domestic or international). External audits can result in gaining QA certification.

quality checks/audits The process where the goods or service are checked either when complete or during the production process to see if the product conforms to the required standard.

quality control The process of implementing a series of checks to see if the product meets internal standards.

reduce A strategy of using fewer resources in the production process.

reuse A strategy of using resources more than once.

recycle A strategy of finding another purpose for a resource.

robotics The use of robots instead of humans to perform work functions.

service providers Businesses that deliver products that are intangible.

services Products that are intangible, that cannot be stored and for which the consumption usually occurs with the purchase, meaning that the consumer is involved directly.

strategies Practices or actions implemented with the aim of achieving a particular effect.

takt An element of lean production that refers to calculating the timing needed to complete items to match the demand from customers.

technology The application of science resulting in machinery and devices.

technology improvements The implementation or upgrade of technology to improve the operations of a business.

Total Quality Management (TQM) A quality system that has the following features:

- a belief in continuous improvement
- an emphasis on teamwork and employee participation to solve quality problems
- customer satisfaction as the main aim.

waste By-products of the production process; the resources that are not put to best use.

waste minimisation Strategies to reduce the amount of waste produced by a business.

zero defects An element of lean production that aims to identify defects at the stage at which they occur to prevent them being carried through to the next stage of the production process.

Revision summary

The first column in the table below has the key knowledge points of Unit 3 Area of Study 3. Read the suggestions in the second column for ways that you can complete notes that will be useful for preparation for both School-assessed Coursework tasks as well as your end-of-year exam.

Unit 3 Area of Study 3 Operations management	Suggestions for summary notes
The relationship between operations management and business objectives	Explain the relationship in a single sentence. (There is an example in Section 3.1.1 that you can check your note against).
Key elements of an operations system: inputs, processes and outputs	Define each term and write an example from a manufacturer that you studied and one example from a service provider for each key element.
Characteristics of operations management within both manufacturing and service businesses	Explain the differences between manufacturing goods and providing services. Outline how each would conduct its operations.
Strategies to improve both the efficiency and effectiveness of operations related to technological developments, including the use of automated production lines, robotics, computer-aided design, computer-aided manufacturing techniques, artificial intelligence and online services	Define efficiency and effectiveness. Here is the tricky bit for all of these operations strategies (technological, materials, quality, waste minimisation and lean management). Some of them will benefit effectiveness, some of them will benefit efficiency and some will benefit both. So for each of these, explain what it means, provide an example of a business that would find it useful and state whether it is more likely to benefit effectiveness, efficiency or both! It's quite a lot to do, but it's worth it because you will be less likely to generalise if you get an exam question on this.
Strategies to improve both the efficiency and effectiveness of operations related to materials, including forecasting, master production schedule, materials requirement planning and Just in Time	For each of these, explain what it means, provide an example of a business that would find it useful and state whether it is more likely to benefit effectiveness, efficiency or both!
Strategies to improve both the efficiency and effectiveness of operations related to quality, including quality control, quality assurance and Total Quality Management	First, make sure you can clearly define the term quality and provide an example. For the three quality strategies, explain what each one means, provide an example of a business that would find it useful and state whether it is more likely to benefit effectiveness, efficiency or both.
Strategies to improve the efficiency and effectiveness of operations through waste minimisation in the production process, including reduce, reuse, recycle	Familiarise yourself with a business that endorses the reduce, reuse, recycle process and use them as an example for your notes. Again, be able to clearly state how this strategy can improve efficiency and, separately, how it can improve effectiveness. Read your notes and make sure that they don't sound too much like materials management or lean management. These strategies are closely related, so be precise and clear. ››

›› The pull, one-piece flow, takt, zero defects strategy to improve the efficiency and effectiveness of operations related to lean management	Although this is worded slightly differently from the previous strategies, it is really similar. Be able to define lean management and explain why businesses undertake it. Explain briefly what each of these four lean strategies mean.
	If you find that your notes start sounding like materials management or waste minimisation, don't forget that lean does not just refer to physical inputs. Lean also refers to processes and it can be useful to keep in mind the different types of waste that lean is designed to minimise.
	Provide an example of how lean management could benefit a manufacturer, then provide a second example of how lean management principles could benefit a service provider.
Corporate social responsibility considerations for an operations system, including the environmental sustainability of inputs and the amount of waste generated from processes and production of outputs	Provide two examples for each of the key elements in terms of corporate social responsibility.
Global considerations for operations management, including global sourcing of inputs, overseas manufacture and global outsourcing	Make sure you use your class notes to assist you here. For each one, explain what it means and provide an example. DO NOT guess. Make sure you are really clear about the differences between all of these terms.

Exam practice

Solutions for this section start on page 105.

Question 1 (1 mark) ⬤○○

Define 'operations management'.

Question 2 (1 mark) ⬤○○

Which of the following would not be considered an input for a car manufacturer?

A steel   **B** workers   **C** welding   **D** tyres

Question 3 (1 mark) ⬤○○

Which of the following would not be considered a process for a five-star hotel?

A cleaning   **B** cooking   **C** mixing drinks   **D** computers

Question 4 (1 mark) ⬤○○

Which of the following would not be considered an output of a fast-food store?

A hamburgers   **B** cooking   **C** fries   **D** shakes

Question 5 (2 marks) ⬤⬤○

'Operations management is really only important for the production of goods.' Is this statement true or false? Explain why.

Question 6 (4 marks) ⬤⬤○

Explain whether the materials requirement plan (MRP) or the master production schedule (MPS) should be developed first.

Question 7 (2 marks) ⬤⬤○

Outline a problem that is associated with the implementation of 'Just in Time' materials management.

Question 8 (2 marks) ⬤⬤⬤

Why would the implementation of ISO 9001:2015 be useful for a service provider?

Question 9 (3 marks) ⬤⬤○

List three features of Total Quality Management.

Question 10 (2 marks) ⬤⬤○

Explain how adopting lean management can assist a business to become more efficient.

Question 11 (1 mark) ⬤○○

Define 'environmental sustainability'.

Question 12 (2 marks) ⬤⬤○

List two ways a business can reduce the waste created in the production process, using an example.

Question 13 (2 marks) ⬤⬤○

Describe one advantage and one disadvantage of sourcing inputs from another country.

Question 14 (4 marks) ⬤⬤⬤

Compare robotics and artificial intelligence.

Question 15 (2 marks) ⬤⬤○

Outline the main advantage of outsourcing manufacturing using a real business example.

Question 16 (3 marks) ⓒVCAA 2017 SB Q2 ●●●

Based on the case study, explain a strategy that Shandra's Dairy Ltd could use to improve the efficiency and effectiveness of its operations in relation to materials.

CASE STUDY

The following is the first page from the 2017 'Report to Shareholders' of Shandra's Dairy Ltd.

Commencing as a family-run business 15 years ago, we are now one of the largest independent dairies in Australia. We are proud of the fact that our raw materials are sourced from local suppliers and that customer satisfaction remains at the centre of our operations. We use a strict quality control strategy to maintain the overall excellence of our products.

Business highlights in 2017
- Market share increased from 15% to 17%
- Increase in volume of sales to over 10 million litres of ice-cream
- Installation of four modern wind turbines at a total cost of $1.25 million, reducing carbon emissions by 3500 tonnes per year, thus assisting us in meeting our 2020 renewable energy target
- A saving of $500 000 per year on electricity bills due to the installation of 600 solar panels

One of our key objectives is to enhance levels of environmental sustainability and make our entire site self-sufficient through renewable energy. Our CEO, Johanna Taylor, is eager to ensure that over 23% of the electricity used comes from renewable sources by 2020. This fits in with the Australian Government's Renewable Energy Target.

'Our commitment to renewable energy has meant an increase in expenses and debt in the short term, but shareholders will continue to see value as the saving in electricity costs will be sustained into the future.'

— Johanna Taylor

Another objective is to become a truly global brand – to do this we need to diversify. Our aim is to launch into the snack food market, concentrating on potato chips. These can be produced at our present manufacturing plant and with the use of our existing suppliers. We believe that this could commence by 2020 and we could export to markets in over 20 countries.

Future goals
- Implement a second strategy to improve quality by 1 July 2018
- Diversify into the snack food market within the next three years

Question 17 (6 marks) ©VCAA 2018 SB Q2 ●●●

Based on the case study, describe the key elements of Ocean Skate Hub's operations system.

The *Daily Swell* is a local print and online newspaper. It recently published the following article about a local business.

Regional community hub for all

Tessa Adams and Charlie Liu opened Ocean Skate Hub in 2017. It is a social enterprise aimed at servicing the needs of the local youth community. It offers indoor and outdoor skate parks, and youth and homework clubs. It also operates a sports shop and café.

After finishing school, Charlie completed a Sports Management degree and Tessa completed a Commerce degree. Having both worked in their chosen fields for several years, Tessa and Charlie recently moved from the city back to their hometown, where they began setting up their business enterprise. Charlie commented that 'we wanted to offer a place where young people from the community could come and try different activities, socialise and gain some new skills'.

After carrying out their research into what financial assistance was available, Tessa and Charlie applied for support through a government initiative called Social Enterprise Finance Australia (SEFA).

SEFA provides finance solutions to mission-led organisations and is deeply committed to fostering positive social and environmental impacts in communities across Australia. SEFA is also there to help new business ventures, like Ocean Skate Hub, build their capacity to manage debt and become financially sustainable.

'We highly value the intensive support we received from SEFA. They helped us put together a rock-solid business case', said Tessa.

Ocean Skate Hub uses its website and social media to provide information to customers and has launched an app to let members book activity sessions. Members are encouraged to give feedback to the organisation to help it meet its aims of improving customer service and finding interesting activities for all users.

All employees are from the local area, and Tessa and Charlie are passionate about keeping all services within the region. Their preference is for staff training to be carried out within the business; however, this is proving to be challenging for Ocean Skate Hub to achieve, and Tessa and Charlie feel they may have to outsource staff training in the future.

With the success of the business behind them, Tessa and Charlie have big plans for expansion in 2019 to provide services for the whole community, not just its youth. These include IT classes for the elderly, as well as photography, cooking, woodwork and gardening classes for all ages.

'With all these exciting changes planned for 2019, we will be relaunching as "Ocean Hub" to better reflect the expanded range of community activities that will soon be available', Charlie said.

Mayor Colin Sprey commented that 'it is encouraging to see our young entrepreneurs giving back to their community'.

Question 18 (4 marks) ©VCAA 2019 SA Q1b ●●

ChocYum Pty Ltd is a manufacturing business located in regional New South Wales. It prides itself on manufacturing chocolate products of the finest quality for major retailers in Australia, New Zealand and the United Kingdom.

Compare the characteristics of operations management within a manufacturing business (such as ChocYum Pty Ltd) with those of a service business.

Question 19 (3 marks) ©VCAA 2020 SA Q5a ●●●

Chef@Home aims to transform the way people prepare meals in their homes. The business delivers all the ingredients required to cook a meal, in a chilled box, to customers' homes. Chef@Home is committed to minimising its carbon footprint, especially through the elimination of waste. All boxes, bags and containers used by the business are recyclable. Ingredients are prepared and packaged using automated production lines. Chef@Home has a policy of sourcing all inputs from local suppliers. Forecasting is a key component of its business operations. At times, Chef@Home's local suppliers have been unable to source and deliver orders placed by the business. Consequently, Chef@Home is considering whether to source some ingredients from overseas suppliers.

Explain an appropriate operations management strategy that Chef@Home could introduce to minimise waste.

Question 20 (4 marks) ©VCAA 2020 SA Q5b ●●

Analyse how forecasting might be used by Chef@Home to improve the efficiency and effectiveness of its operations.

Exam practice: Case study

Solutions for this section start on page 108.

CASE STUDY

Thunder Sportswear began in the 1970s when Billy Bunting won a competition to design netball and football uniforms for his school. When he left school, Billy did a design course. On completing the course, he set up a small workshop in his hometown of Creswick, initially just supplying local teams in Bendigo and Ballarat. In 2022 Billy had two factories in close proximity in Ballarat. One concentrates on the manufacture of football jumpers and the other produces casual clothing ranges. Thunder Sportswear has just started manufacturing retro footy jumpers made of wool, which are selling well to the hipster market. The wool fabric is sourced from local producers in Victoria but is more expensive than similar fabrics sourced from overseas. Billy is proud to be able to state that the entire product is Australian made. He is hoping to soon expand to making basketball uniforms with the American and Japanese markets in mind.

Questions

Question 1 (3 marks) ●○○

Define inputs and provide two examples of inputs for Thunder Sportswear.

Question 2 (3 marks) ●○○

Define processes and provide two examples of processes that would be completed at Thunder Sportswear.

Question 3 (2 marks) ●○○

Explain the relationship between operations management and business objectives.

Question 4 (2 marks) ●○○

Distinguish between goods and services.

Question 5 (1 + 2 + 2 = 5 marks) ⬤⬤▨

Customers have started complaining that the woollen retro-style footy jumpers shrink by four sizes after washing. The colours also run when they are washed. The fabric that is used to produce the jumpers was ordered in large amounts, so now there is a fear that Thunder has a large amount of stock that might all be faulty. An emergency meeting has been scheduled by the operations manager, Jacqui Chang, where the following data will be discussed.

KPI	% change over the past 6 months
Customer complaints	↑ 25%
Sales of retro jumpers	↓ 10%
Market share	↓ 15%
Levels of waste	↑ 10%

Identify and describe one materials strategy that would be useful to Thunder Sportswear in this situation and justify your choice.

Question 6 (2 marks) ⬤⬤▨

Identify and describe one performance indicator that would be appropriate to assess if the strategy you selected in question 5 was successful. Justify your choice.

Question 7 (6 marks) ⬤⬤⬤

Discuss whether quality control or quality assurance would be more effective for Thunder Sportswear to resolve its quality problems.

Question 8 (4 marks) ⬤⬤▨

Identify and describe one technology strategy that could increase efficiency at Thunder Sportswear.

Question 9 (4 marks) ⬤⬤▨

Jacqui Chang is considering implementing lean production methods to combat the increase in the level of waste. Explain what is meant by 'lean production' and how it could be of assistance at Thunder Sportswear.

Question 10 (6 marks) ⬤⬤⬤

Billy and Jacqui are considering whether they might need to purchase their fabric from an overseas supplier. Evaluate whether this strategy would be advantageous to Thunder Sportswear.

Question 11 (3 marks) ⬤⬤▨

Explain one corporate social responsibility consideration that Thunder Sportswear could incorporate in terms of its operations.

Total = 40 marks

UNIT 4
TRANSFORMING A BUSINESS

Chapter 4

Area of Study 1: Reviewing performance
– the need for change 65

Chapter 5

Area of Study 2: Implementing change 79

Chapter 4
Area of Study 1: Reviewing performance – the need for change

Area of Study summary

The premise for this area of study is that businesses do not remain static. In order to gain or maintain a competitive edge, managers need to employ proactive and/or reactive strategies and would use a review of their key performance indicators (KPIs) to understand their position in the market.

You will need to understand Lewin's Force Field Analysis and how driving and restraining forces determine the ease with which a change process may be implemented.

Finally, you will look at two possible change options for businesses seeking a competitive advantage: Porter's cost leadership or differentiation strategies.

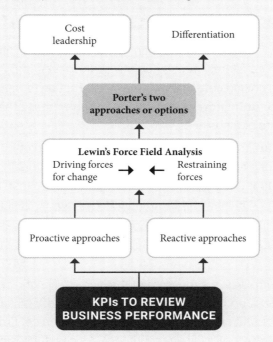

Area of Study 1 Outcome 1

On completing this outcome you should be able to:

- explain the way business change may come about
- analyse why managers may take a **proactive** or **reactive** approach to change
- use key performance indicators to analyse the performance of a business
- explain the **driving and restraining forces** for change
- evaluate management strategies to position a business for the future.

The key skills demonstrated in this outcome are:

- identify, define, describe and apply business management concepts and terms
- interpret, discuss, compare and evaluate business information, theories and ideas
- analyse case studies and contemporary examples of business management
- apply business management knowledge to practical and/or simulated business situations
- propose, justify and evaluate management strategies to improve business performance.

VCE Business Management Study Design 2023–2027 pp. 22–23, © VCAA 2022

4.1   Business change

4.1.1 Proactive and reactive approaches to change

It would be a very unusual business that did not undertake some form of change. **Business change** can be defined as the process of altering some aspects of the organisation to create a new form of them.

Change can be undertaken as a proactive or reactive approach. Neither is necessarily better than the other; indeed businesses usually need to do both. Being **proactive** means that the **managers** are making changes to improve the business in anticipation of what might be ahead. They may be trend-setting in terms of product development or improved processes. Being proactive can keep a business ahead of its **competitors** and ensure that valuable **employees** will want to stay. A **reactive** approach, however, may be necessary if something has gone wrong or was unforeseen. There may be an internal problem to fix or the business may find that competitors have the edge and they need to catch up.

4.1.2 Key performance indicators to analyse performance

So how do those in charge of a business know when it's the right time to introduce change?

Managers and owners are constantly monitoring the performance of their businesses. If they are not achieving their goals, it might indicate that it's time to take action (a reactive approach as just explained). **Key performance indicators (KPIs)** are measurable criteria that can be used to evaluate the success and achievements of a business.

- *Percentage of* **market share** (don't mix this up with the share market!): This is the percentage of **sales** or business that one firm has compared with its competitors in the same industry. For example, it might be said that Coca-Cola has a larger market share than Pepsi, but that these two dominate the cola market. Successful firms would aim to increase their market share.

- *Net* **profit** *figures*: Net profit is the amount of income left when expenses are deducted from a business's revenue. A successful business would be making a profit, or even better, increasing its profit.

- *Rate of* **productivity** *growth*: This is a measure of the increases in the amount of output per given amount of inputs per period of time. It's a basic measure of efficiency. Labour productivity measures the amount of output per worker (or labour unit) over a set time period, while multifactor productivity also adds the effect of capital resources. A successful business should have productivity levels that tend to increase over time.

- *Number of sales*: This KPI is closely related to market share. It is a simple numerical measure of how many sales the business has made in a time period. Businesses would be keen to maximise the number of sales within the limits of the production capacity.

- *Rates of* **staff absenteeism**: This means the rate at which employees are taking days off work. This can be for a number of reasons such as sick leave or carer's leave. In many enterprise agreements, this comes under the category of personal leave. In some cases it may reflect dissatisfaction at work, or worse, bullying or other issues. In such cases managers would need to determine the cause and try to rectify the situation.

- *Level of* **staff turnover**: This is the rate at which staff leave and are replaced within a business. If the staff turnover rate is high, it could indicate a problem with some aspects of the business. A process of conducting exit interviews may be a good strategy to identify the cause of a high staff turnover rate.

- *Level of wastage*: This refers to surplus, excess, damaged or unused resources. This is another way to measure efficiency. It does not just refer to raw materials in manufacturing, but to the waste of any resources, including labour, time and money. If this is a problem, adopting lean or **waste** minimisation principles could prove to be effective. (See Chapter 3.)

- *Number of* **customer complaints**: This is the number of times that customers have expressed dissatisfaction with a business and its goods and/or services. If customers are not happy, they are usually prepared to let the business know. Their methods of complaining can vary from phone calls, to talking to staff members in person, sending emails or just expressing their unhappiness on social media sites.

- *Number of* **website hits**: Businesses keep track of how effective their online presence is through measures such as the number of times that people access their websites and social media sites. This can tell them if they are visible when potential customers are searching for similar products and whether they need to change their online strategy.

- *Number of* **workplace accidents**: This reflects the number of times that someone is injured or becomes ill as a consequence of some aspect at work. Obviously a zero figure for this KPI would be best, but some industries require dangerous work to be performed (e.g. mining). If the number of workplace accidents decreases, it would be a sign that safety policies are working effectively for the business.

Triple bottom line accounting

An increasingly popular method of determining if a business is doing well is the triple bottom line (TBL or 3BL) accounting approach where a business is assessed in terms of:

- economic factors (financial)
- social factors
- environmental factors.

It is felt that this provides a balanced picture of the success of an organisation rather than just looking at one indicator.

Industry-specific KPIs

While this KPI list is general, sometimes there can be other KPIs that are specific to one industry. If we looked at a five-star hotel in Melbourne, a relevant KPI would include the occupancy rate compared with previous years. When analysing KPIs, it doesn't really matter if it's a large or small business. They would all have goals and standards of performance that they want to achieve. A gardening business might want to increase the number of customers it has from one year to the next, hence increasing its market share. Large retail stores might aim to improve their net profit figures. Restaurants might aim to reduce the amount of wastage.

> **Hint**
> If asked to propose a suitable KPI for a situation, make sure that you consider what would be most appropriate. How big is the business? Does it conduct dangerous work? Is it a public company or a social enterprise? If you can narrow down the basic objectives of the business, you should be able to suggest a KPI that is relevant.

> **Hint**
> Search online for the annual reports of government business enterprises such as Australia Post or public companies such as banks. These will provide you with a range of KPIs that are relevant to that business. Often, they state how well the business has performed against specific targets that were set the preceding year.

istock.com/Hispanolistic

4.2 Change management theories

4.2.1 Lewin's Force Field Analysis theory

Once the need for change has been identified, it can be worthwhile to establish what is driving the change and what is restraining it.

Kurt Lewin (1890–1947) was a psychologist who studied group dynamics and organisational development. He developed the **Force Field Analysis** theory, which looked at the factors that are helpful in achieving a goal (**driving forces**) against those that hinder or prevent the achievement of the goal (**restraining forces**) (see Figure 4.1). In order for change to occur, the equilibrium or balance between the two forces must be broken, with the driving forces winning through.

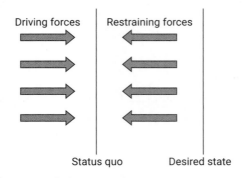

FIGURE 4.1 Lewin's Force Field Analysis theory

It is not the number of driving forces versus the number of restraining forces that determine if change is likely to be successful, however. Some forces are more powerful or have more value than others, so a process needs to be undertaken to determine whether or not the driving forces have the ability to push through the restraining forces.

A process that managers could undertake could look like this.

1. *State the change that is desired.* This may relate to one of the business objectives (proactive) and/or may be in response to recent KPIs (reactive).

2. *Brainstorm the driving forces.* List everything possible that will enable and encourage the change to occur.

3. *Brainstorm the restraining forces.* List everything that could prevent the change from being successful or from even happening at all. What are the obstacles?

4. *Weight the driving and restraining forces.* Some forces will be more powerful than others. These should be assigned greater weight. For example, cost might be the only restraining force, but if the proposed change is unaffordable, then this will have a greater weight than many of the other forces combined.

5. *Rank the driving and restraining forces.* Ranking means to put into priority order, considering a number of factors as well as the weighting. The ranking will come back to the reasons for the change.

6. *Implement a response.* This is the most difficult stage where managers need to determine if there are ways to strengthen the driving forces or weaken the restraining forces to get to the stage where the driving forces can prevail.

7. *Evaluate the response.* All changes should be evaluated to monitor if the change has been successful. If the response determined in step 6 does not appear to be working, then managers will need to decide whether to work further to overcome the restraining forces or if the change should be abandoned.

4.2.2 Driving and restraining forces

Driving forces

Driving forces are factors that apply pressure for changes to occur. Here is a list of some of the most common driving forces for businesses today.

- Owners: If profits are not as great as the owners would like them to be, they may introduce changes to rectify this. Owners have their own money invested, so they want to protect this and build on it. They have the ability to make all decisions, so they are a significant driving force.

- Managers: The desire to introduce changes may come from senior managers or one of the middle managers; for example, an operations manager wanting a different layout to improve efficiency.

- Employees: Employees may initiate changes if there are things that can be introduced to their advantage; for example, demand for family-friendly human resource policies.

- Competitors: If competitors are proving to be more successful, then the business may introduce changes to keep up with or outperform them; for example, they might introduce new technology or change some of their work practices.

- **Legislation**: If the law changes, then businesses are obliged to introduce the required changes. This has been particularly obvious lately in terms of occupational health and safety and the changes to workplace relations.

- Pursuit of profit: If profit levels are not as high as the managers (or shareholders) would like, they may make changes to either generate more revenue or decrease their **costs** to achieve their goals (see reduction of costs below).

- Reduction of costs: Change might be an option if the costs of production are proving to be too expensive; for example, a business may consider outsourcing aspects of its production to save money on labour costs.

- **Globalisation**: Rapid improvements to communication and other forms of technology have broken down trade barriers between countries. The concept of global markets means that an organisation may feel compelled to compete with not just other businesses in the same state or country, but also those around the world. This could entail making changes to the way business is conducted or making better use of the internet and e-commerce.

- **Technology**: Constant improvements to technology can drive a business to make changes to keep up. It is highly unusual for a retailer not to offer online sales today. Most make use of social media as a form of promotion. These are quite recent changes, implemented by businesses to take advantage of improvements in technology. In other cases, it could be advances in electric car technology or businesses storing data in the cloud rather than physically storing it.

- **Innovation**: A tangent from technology as a driving force is innovation. While some innovations are technology based, not all are. The need to innovate could be a driving force in itself. In other cases, businesses may feel pressured to keep up with their competitors' innovations. An example of this is the trend for supermarkets to install self-service checkouts. This is an innovative practice.

- **Societal attitudes**: Society places a great deal of pressure on organisations to implement changes. In recent years, this has taken the form of changes in concern for the environment, recognising that there are more women in the workforce and acknowledging that there are more families where both parents work.

Restraining forces

Restraining forces are factors that repress the pressures for change. They can hinder progress or prevent it from occurring. Here is a list of some examples of restraining forces.

- Managers: While usually the drivers, sometimes managers can be those who resist change. If another stakeholder group (e.g. shareholders or customers) is pushing for change, managers may not believe that it is in the best interests of the business and they may try to ensure that the requested change does not happen.

- Employees: Employees often fear changes. It is often said that the main reason that the implementation of change is not successful is because of **employee resistance**. They may have concerns about their job security and they may fear how it will affect the nature of their jobs. Because of this, they may consciously resist a change by not implementing required new practices or even by sabotaging the changes.

- Time: Even if all stakeholder groups want the change, sometimes there may not be enough time to take advantage of an opportunity.

- **Organisational inertia**: This refers to a state that can develop within a business that is not open and receptive to change. The culture may not allow change to be introduced easily.

- Legislation: There are instances where a government body might actually stop change from happening. For example, the Australian Competition and Consumer Commission (ACCC) can prevent a merger from happening or occupational health and safety laws can prevent a business from undertaking changes that could potentially cause injury to the workers.

- Financial considerations: Sometimes the cost associated with the introduction of change is such that it is just not viable. Organisations sometimes conduct a cost–benefit analysis to see if making the change is really going to be worthwhile.

4.2.3 Porter's Generic Strategies theory

Michael Porter is a professor at the Harvard Business School. In the 1980s, he developed a theory that attempts to explain how businesses can gain a competitive advantage.

When looking to take advantage of their strengths, businesses need to react to the five competitive forces:

- the entry of new competitors
- the threat of substitutes
- the bargaining power of buyers
- the bargaining power of suppliers
- the rivalry among existing competitors.

According to Porter:

> The five forces determine industry profitability because they influence prices, costs and required investment of firms in an industry – the elements of return on investment.

> Buyer power influences the prices that firms can charge, for example, as does the threat of substitution. The power of buyers can also influence cost and investment, because powerful buyers demand costly service.

> The bargaining power of suppliers determines the costs of raw materials and other inputs. The intensity of rivalry influences prices as well as the costs of competing in areas such as plant, product development, advertising and sales force. The threat of entry places a limit on prices, and shapes the investment required to deter entrants.

Porter ME. (2008) *Competitive Advantage: Creating and Sustaining Superior Performance.* Free Press, p. 5.

Porter's theory

Porter's **Generic Strategies theory** relies on an understanding of two concepts.

The first is that this is a generic strategy. In this sense, generic means that it can be applied to any business or industry.

The second is that a business needs to identify and concentrate on its strengths. These are competitive advantages and tend to be in two categories:

- cost advantage
- differentiation.

If the strength is applied to the business, three generic strategies can result: cost leadership, differentiation and focus.

Cost leadership

This is where managers decide that the business will aim to become the lowest cost producer of a product. In order to achieve this, the managers may need to review their materials management strategies or consider the remuneration that is offered to employees. It could involve the implementation of new technology to produce products faster and with less waste, hence reducing the business's costs (including labour costs).

Differentiation

Differentiation is where the business can make their good or service appear to have a unique point of difference from its competitors. According to Porter:

> Differentiation can be based on the product itself, the delivery system by which it is sold, the marketing approach and a broad range of other factors.
>
> Porter ME (2008). *Competitive Advantage: Creating and Sustaining Superior Performance*. Kindle Locations 621–622. Free Press. Kindle Edition.

If this point of difference is valued, their customers may be willing to pay higher prices for this product, rather than those offered by competitors at a lower cost. For example, Apple products are differentiated from their competitors and most luxury goods use this strategy.

Focus

This is where the managers decide to target a narrow segment of the market. It is offering a niche product to that market segment and may be based on either lower cost or differentiation. The aim is to develop a very loyal customer base. An example of this is Gourmet Pawprints, which offers experiences such as winery tours and cinema evenings for people with their dogs. In this case the target market is small and the product is clearly based on differentiation.

Porter's theory and change management

So how does all of this fit in with the concept of change management? Once managers have identified through analysis of relevant KPIs that changes are necessary, they need to decide which strategy is right for them to pursue. The choice of strategy will be aligned with the business's mission and vision statements and their long-term goals. A decision needs to be made about whether to pursue an advantage through lower costs or a differentiated product. Once this decision is made, the managers will be able to focus on making the changes that are required to achieve this.

Hint

Read more on Porter's theory: Porter ME. (2008) *Competitive Advantage: Creating and Sustaining Superior Performance*. Free Press.

Glossary

business change The process that alters the existing state of aspects of a business and creates a new form of them.

competitors Rival businesses that produce similar goods and/or services.

costs Expenses that are incurred by a business.

customer complaints A measure of how many times those who purchase products express their dissatisfaction.

differentiation The process of making a product distinct from other products made by the same producer or those produced by competitors.

driving forces Factors that apply pressure for change to occur.

employee A worker in a business who is paid an income in exchange for their labour.

employee resistance A state that occurs when the workers in a business fight or block a change that is being introduced.

Force Field Analysis A theory developed by Lewin that states that driving forces must push through restraining forces if change is to occur.

Generic Strategies theory A system of improving performance by focusing on minimising costs and/or differentiating the product in order to gain an advantage over rivals.

globalisation Rapid improvements to communication and technology resulting in fewer trade barriers between countries.

innovation The development of something new, either a product or a production technique.

key performance indicators (KPIs) Criteria that can be used to evaluate the success and achievements of an organisation.

legislation A law or a set of laws that have been passed by Parliament.

managers Those in leadership positions who have responsibility for a section of a business.

market share The percentage of sales or business that one firm has compared with its competitors in the same industry.

A+ DIGITAL FLASHCARDS
Revise this topic's key terms and concepts by scanning the QR code or typing the URL into your browser.

https://get.ga/aplus-vce-busmgmt-u34

organisational inertia A state that can develop within a business that is not open and receptive to change.

Porter's theory See Generic Strategies theory.

proactive Making changes in anticipation of what might occur.

productivity The amount of output that can be produced with a given set of inputs over a period of time.

profit The amount of income left over when expenses are deducted from revenue.

reactive Making changes in response to something that has occurred.

restraining forces Factors that repress or block pressures for change.

sales The number of purchases made by customers.

societal attitudes Commonly held values and points of view.

staff absenteeism The rate at which staff are taking days off work.

staff turnover The rate at which staff leave and are replaced in a business.

technology The application of science resulting in machinery and devices.

website hits The number of times people access files or visit a website.

waste By-products of the production process; the resources that are not put to best use.

workplace accidents Situations where employees are injured while at work.

9780170465137

Revision summary

The first column in the table below has the key knowledge points of Unit 4 Area of Study 1. Read the suggestions in the second column for ways that you can complete notes that will be useful for preparation for both School-assessed Coursework tasks as well as your end-of-year exam.

Unit 4 Area of Study 1 Transforming a business	Suggestions for summary notes
The concept of business change	Explain what this concept means and provide one real example.
Proactive and reactive approaches to change	Define each term and provide a real business example of each.
Key performance indicators as sources of data to analyse the performance of businesses, percentage of market share, net profit figures, rate of productivity growth, number of sales, rates of staff absenteeism, level of staff turnover, level of wastage, number of customer complaints, number of website hits and number of workplace accidents	Define the term key performance indicator (KPI). Now define each of the listed KPIs and state whether it is better for the figure to be high or low. Make sure you also know which should be expressed in whole numbers and which should be expressed as a percentage increase or decrease.
Key principles of the Force Field Analysis theory (Lewin) including weighting, ranking, implementing a response and evaluating the response	Explain how the Force Field Analysis theory works. Include a diagram with all these stages if you would find it helpful.
Driving forces for change in business including owners, managers, employees, competitors, legislation, pursuit of profit, reduction of costs, globalisation, technology, innovation and societal attitudes	Define 'driving forces' for change. For each of the driving forces listed, give an example of how it could be a driving force, such as: 'For example, managers may drive a change such as merging with another business if they think that it will make the business more successful'. Make sure that your legislation example includes an actual law. Make sure you have a definition of globalisation here as well as the example. Be specific with the technology. What sort are you talking about? Make sure you have a real example of innovation. Go back to your class notes and/or textbook to assist you. If possible, use an example that is not technology based to differentiate it from technology as a driving force. Make sure you clearly state which societal attitude(s) you mean in your example. Be quite specific.
Restraining forces in businesses, including managers, employees, time, organisational inertia, legislation and financial considerations	Define 'restraining forces'. Do the same thing for these examples as you did for the driving forces. Be very specific in your examples here as well. Be sure that you have a definition of 'organisational inertia' that you can elaborate on in your own words.
The two key approaches (lower cost and differentiation) to strategic management according to Porter's Generic Strategies	Explain what each approach means and provide a real business example of each one.

VCE Business Management Study Design 2023–2027 p. 22, © VCAA 2022

CHAPTER 4 – REVISION SUMMARY

Exam practice

Solutions for this section start on page 109.

Question 1 (2 marks) ⬤◯⬤

Explain why businesses monitor their performance.

Question 2 (1 mark) ◯⬤⬤

Identify a business that would need to carefully monitor the number of workplace accidents.

Question 3 (1 + 2 = 3 marks) ◯⬤⬤

Propose and justify a KPI that would be appropriate for a supermarket.

Question 4 (3 marks) ⬤⬤⬤

Is it possible for a business to increase the number of sales, but reduce its net profit? Explain your answer.

Question 5 (4 marks) ⬤⬤◯

Compare the concepts of staff absenteeism rates and staff turnover rates.

Question 6 (2 marks) ⬤⬤◯

Outline Lewin's Force Field Analysis theory.

Question 7 (2 marks) ⬤⬤◯

List two examples of how employees could be the driving force behind change.

Question 8 (4 marks) ⬤⬤⬤

Explain how the pursuit of profit can be a slightly different driving force from the reduction in costs.

Question 9 (1 mark) ◯⬤⬤

Define 'restraining forces'.

Question 10 (2 marks) ◯⬤⬤

List two reasons why employees might resist change.

Question 11 (2 marks) ⬤⬤◯

Explain 'competitive advantage'.

Question 12 (5 marks) ◯⬤⬤

List the five competitive forces as stated by Porter.

Question 13 (2 marks) ⬤⬤◯

Identify one advantage and one disadvantage of a business prioritising cost leadership as its strategy.

Question 14 (2 marks) ⬤⬤◯

Identify two examples of businesses that have differentiated their products to the point where customers are willing to pay higher prices for them.

Question 15 (2 marks) ◯⬤⬤

'The focus strategy is applied to a very broad market.' Is this statement true or false?

Question 16 (4 marks)   ©VCAA 2017 SB Q6   ●○○

One of the objectives of Shandra's Dairy Ltd (see the case study below) is to become a truly global brand. Explain **one** driving force and **one** restraining force that could have an impact on the success of this objective.

CASE STUDY

The following is the first page from the 2017 'Report to Shareholders' of Shandra's Dairy Ltd.

Commencing as a family-run business 15 years ago, we are now one of the largest independent dairies in Australia. We are proud of the fact that our raw materials are sourced from local suppliers and that customer satisfaction remains at the centre of our operations. We use a strict quality control strategy to maintain the overall excellence of our products.

Business highlights in 2017

- Market share increased from 15% to 17%
- Increase in volumes of sales to over 10 million litres of ice-cream
- Installation of four modern wind turbines at a total cost of $1.25 million, reducing carbon emissions by 3500 tonnes per year, thus assisting us in meeting our 2020 renewable energy target
- A saving of $500 000 per year on electricity bills due to the installation of 600 solar panels

One of our key objectives is to enhance levels of environmental sustainability and make our entire site self-sufficient through renewable energy. Our CEO, Johanna Taylor, is eager to ensure that over 23% of the electricity used comes from renewable sources by 2020. This fits in with the Australian Government's Renewable Energy Target.

Our commitment to renewable energy has meant an increase in expenses and debt in the short term, but shareholders will continue to see value as the saving in electricity costs will be sustained into the future.

— Johanna Taylor

Another objective is to become a truly global brand – to do this we need to diversify. Our aim is to launch into the snack food market, concentrating on potato chips. These can be produced at our present manufacturing plant and with the use of our existing suppliers. We believe that this could commence by 2020 and we could export to markets in over 20 countries.

Future goals

- Implement a second strategy to improve quality by 1 July 2018
- Diversify into the snack food market within the next three years

Question 17 (6 marks)   ©VCAA 2018 SA Q2   ●●○

Explain the importance of leadership in change management. In your response, refer to a contemporary business case study.

Question 18 (4 marks)   ©VCAA 2019 SA Q5b   ●●●

Dennis Greeves is the manager of a highly successful, Melbourne-based burger chain. In response to a decline in sales and a change in customer tastes, Dennis has made the decision to implement a policy of using only ethically sourced, high-quality local ingredients. Dennis is aware that a new pricing strategy will be required as a result and that the Executive Chef will require support to implement the changes.

Analyse how Dennis has used Porter's Generic Strategies to respond to the issues of declining sales and changing customer tastes.

Question 19 (4 marks)   ©VCAA 2019 SA Q2   ●●○

Managers can take either a proactive or a reactive approach to change. Describe how each of these approaches can be used to manage change.

Question 20 (6 marks) ©VCAA | VCAA 2020 SB Q4 | ●●●

Based on the following case study, other than those named in the extract of the speech delivered by the Chief Executive Officer, explain two KPIs that Manitta Mining could use to assess business performance.

CASE STUDY

Below is an extract of a speech delivered to the shareholders of Manitta Mining by its Chief Executive Officer at its annual general meeting on 7 August 2020.

Our business faces significant challenges. Staff turnover has increased significantly over a five-year period. The business's share price on the Australian Securities Exchange (ASX) has decreased by 15% over the same five-year period. Sales are also down and the company has struggled to reduce the number of workplace accidents in our mines.

As Chief Executive Officer of Manitta Mining for more than 15 years, I am pleased to tell you the long-term outlook for the company remains strong. Since the appointment of a new operations manager, Dr Margaret Sherckle, in February 2020, the number of workplace accidents has decreased by 25%. The number of workplace accidents is a very important key performance indicator (KPI) for the business and a key business objective is to improve workplace safety.

Manitta Mining currently has more than 20 000 employees, each of whom I consider to be part of the 'Manitta family'. While business efficiency and effectiveness are important, the goal of ensuring that our employees return home safely each day is our priority.

A safe workplace will reduce staff turnover. It will also reduce staff absenteeism. We aim to keep staff turnover below 5% in the year ahead. This will reduce associated costs. For example, reduced staff turnover will reduce staff training costs. WorkCover premiums will also fall. Manitta Mining expects that increased employee retention will lead to significant increases in the rate of productivity growth during the next 12 months.

Finally, I would like to thank you, the shareholders. Loyalty deserves to be rewarded. The implementation of strategies that improve business performance through increased productivity growth will ensure that your investment grows in turn.

Thank you.

Exam practice: Case study A

Solutions for this section start on page 112.

Pretty Pooches is a chain of dog grooming and accessory shops owned by Anouk Mawson. Her business has grown steadily over the past 10 years, but some recent data has concerned her.

CASE
STUDY
A

Photo courtesy of Debra McNaughton

KPI	Change over the past year
Net profit	↑ 20%
Number of customer complaints	↓ 10%
Staff turnover	↑ 25%
Number of workplace accidents (mainly due to dog bites)	↑ 30%

Anouk must now make some decisions about the future of her business.

Questions

Question 1 (3 marks) ●○○

Define the following terms:

a restraining forces

b staff turnover rate

c profit.

Question 2 (6 marks) ●●○

Apply Lewin's Force Field Analysis theory to Pretty Pooches in relation to the data provided.

Question 3 (8 marks) ●●●

Discuss how both legislation and the pursuit of profit could be driving forces for change in this situation.

Question 4 (2 marks) ●○○

Explain how financial considerations can be a restraining force.

Question 5 (6 marks) ●●●

Evaluate whether Pretty Pooches would be better off pursuing lower cost options or differentiation as described by Porter's theory.

Total = 25 marks

Exam practice: Case study B

Solutions for this section start on page 113.

Solutions for this section start on page 113.

CASE STUDY B	A social enterprise called Eduk8ed was established in 2005. It sells a range of stationery items such as notebooks, diaries and pencils that are ethically sourced from a range of communities. The profits are directed to providing school uniforms and books for students in need in Australia. In recent years, Eduk8ed has been able to maintain a high level of sales compared with popular stationery businesses, yet profit is falling. The CEO, Ian Indigo, is working through the options.

KPI	Change over the past year
Net profit	↓ 45%
Market share	↓ 20%
Number of sales	↑ 5%

Questions

Question 1 (1 mark) ●○○

Define 'business change'.

Question 2 (4 marks) ●●○

Explain the key principles of Lewin's Force Field Analysis theory.

Question 3 (4 marks) ●●○

Propose two driving forces for change based on the data provided.

Question 4 (4 marks) ●●○

Compare Porter's concepts of differentiation and lower cost.

Question 5 (4 marks) ●●●

Ian Indigo has found that much of the stock was not sold over the past year, so that the level of waste was high. Discuss whether this is a concern if the profit levels remain high.

Question 6 (6 marks) ●●○

Ian decides to pursue a strategy of lower costs. Explain, in relation to Eduk8ed, how employees and organisational inertia could both be restraining forces that prevent or slow the process of change.

Question 7 (2 marks) ●●○

Explain how it is possible that the number of sales increased by 5% yet the net profit decreased by 45%.

Total = 25 marks

Chapter 5
Area of Study 2: Implementing change

Area of Study summary

Once the business managers have decided that change is necessary, they need a way to implement it smoothly, and that is what this area of study is all about. After reviewing the key performance indicators (KPIs; see Chapter 4), managers need strategies to set the business on the desired course. Depending on the urgency of the change, they may implement low-risk or high-risk strategies to move through the stages of change as described by Lewin.

Corporate culture is described in Chapter 1; however, here you will learn how to develop the desired culture and why a positive culture is necessary when implementing change. This is linked to Senge's concept of a Learning Organisation.

There are two considerations for managers when implementing change that are addressed in this area of study: (a) the effect on stakeholders; and (b) corporate social responsibility effects of the change and/or change process.

Finally, you will learn that this cycle of improvement is ongoing. Managers need to go back to the KPIs to see if the change has been successful and if the business's objectives are being achieved (from Chapter 1).

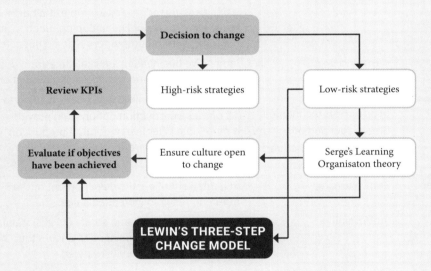

Area of Study 2 Outcome 2

On completing this outcome, you should be able to:

- discuss the importance of effective management **strategies** and leadership in relation to change
- evaluate the effectiveness of a variety of strategies used by managers to implement change
- discuss the effect of change on the stakeholders of a business.

The key skills demonstrated in this outcome are:

- identify, define, describe and apply business management concepts and terms
- interpret, discuss, compare and evaluate business information, theories and ideas
- analyse case studies and contemporary examples of business management
- apply business management knowledge to practical and/or simulated business situations
- propose, justify and evaluate management strategies to improve business performance.

VCE Business Management Study Design 2023–2027 pp. 23–24, © VCAA 2022

5.1 Leading change

5.1.1 Leadership in change management

Leadership is very important during a period of change. If strong leadership qualities can be employed, more trust will be generated among **employees**, leading to less resistance to change. This can allow the transformation process to occur more quickly and with a greater possibility of success.

5.1.2 Management strategies to respond to KPIs

Managers constantly monitor **key performance indicators (KPIs)** and respond when it appears that the business is not heading in the direction that the managers would like. (Refer back to Chapter 4.) Table 5.1 includes some of the more common **strategies** that managers might implement to get the business back on track. Please note that the strategies can assist in improving many of the KPIs. The strategies have just been linked with one or two KPIs here to illustrate the ways they can benefit the business.

KPIs that can be addressed	Management strategy	Examples of the relationships between the strategies and KPIs
Percentage of market share	Increased investment in: • **technology**	Installing better technology than competitors can give a business the edge. For example, if a business has a really easy-to-use online shopping function, it may pick up customers from competitors who do not offer this option.
	• **innovation**	Innovative businesses are likely to attract customers from their competitors, hence increasing market share.
Net profit figures	Initiating **lean production** techniques Global sourcing of **inputs** Overseas manufacture Global **outsourcing**	Lean production will reduce costs, leading to greater profit. All of these production options can provide a business with a more cost-effective method of production, which can lead to increased profit.
Number of sales	Staff **training**	In a retail situation, the development of the skills of sales staff can result in increased sales.
Number of workplace accidents	Staff training	Occupational health and safety (OH&S) training is necessary in every business to ensure that the incidence of accidents and injury is reduced.
Level of staff turnover or staff absenteeism	Change in **management styles** or **management skills**	In some cases an autocratic management style may not be seen by employees as desirable. If employees are resigning or taking many days off because they don't feel involved or even consulted about decisions at work, then a change to a consultative or participative style might be required. This would also require the development of better communication and interpersonal skills.
Rate of productivity growth	Increased investment in technology	Technology can also assist with increasing the rate of productivity as it may assist the business to produce items more quickly while retaining accuracy and quality.
Customer complaints	Improving **quality** in production	The implementation of a quality strategy such as quality assurance systems (see Chapter 3) should result in better quality products. This should see the number of complaints from customers decrease.

KPIs that can be addressed	Management strategy	Examples of the relationships between the strategies and KPIs
Profit	Cost cutting	Profit is not just based on the revenue earned by a business. A business can increase its profit margins if it retains its revenue levels, but reduces its costs. This can be done by sourcing less-expensive inputs. In a restaurant, for example, cost cutting could be achieved by finding a less-expensive butcher to supply the meat.
Rate of productivity growth	Staff motivation	When motivation levels are increased, employees are more likely to work hard, thus increasing the productivity rate.
Level of wastage	Initiation of lean production techniques	Lean production is based on the concept of minimising waste. (See Chapter 3 for a list of the types of waste.) By making the most of all resources, the business will minimise its waste levels. It will also reduce its costs (see the strategy above).
For many KPIs	Redeployment of **capital resources**, **labour resources** and **natural resources**	Depending on which KPIs the managers want to improve, the solution might be to place resources into more effective positions or processes within the business. For example, maybe more employees are needed in the section of the business that is growing most strongly. Or perhaps more capital resources in the form of equipment needs to be taken from under-performing areas to produce the items that are most in demand.

TABLE 5.1 Examples of relationships between KPIs and management strategies

5.1.3 Management strategies to seek new business opportunities

If the managers decide to expand the business and increase their market share, they may look for new business opportunities. These can be within Australia (domestic market) or globally.

- Differentiating the product: New **customers** may be attracted by making the product (whether it is a good or a service) different from the competitor's product. State governments can assist businesses to find business opportunities. Business Victoria not only offers advice for businesses, but also offers financial assistance in some cases. An example of this is the Future Industries Manufacturing Program, which offers up to $500 000 to Victorian businesses in order to assist them to implement new technology and/or technological-based processes.

- By seeking new global opportunities, businesses can dramatically increase their customer bases. Knowing how to do this can be daunting. This is where the services provided by Austrade can benefit businesses. Through Austrade, Australian companies can access information about trading internationally. Austrade focuses on supporting businesses that aim to export to countries that are not already established markets for Australia. Accessing the services provided by Austrade can be a very effective strategy for businesses wanting to tap into global markets.

Hint
Have a look at the Austrade website to read about the assistance that is currently available for businesses that want to seek new global opportunities.

5.1.4 Management strategies to develop corporate culture

If the real **corporate culture** does not reflect the desired or official culture, managers may implement strategies to try to make the workplace more positive, industrious or supportive. Here are some ways that managers can do this.

- Recruit employees with the desired attitudes. If the attributes of the culture are written into job descriptions, and if selection interviews address these, all new staff will already demonstrate the desired culture.

- Communicate the desired culture to all stakeholders. It may be the case that the employees are unaware of what the business managers are trying to achieve. Clear, effective **communication** (which includes listening) can improve the culture.

- Empower employees. If employees are able to make some decisions on their own, they may take ownership of the business's decisions, and hence take more pride in the outcomes. This can assist in creating a more positive industrious culture.

- Team-building activities. These can be low-key, such as group work projects, or involve weekends away doing paintball or other team-based activities. The relationships and trust that develop can be reflected in all other aspects of workplace activities.

- Change the style of management. If the business operates with autocratic managers, and the culture is not positive, then perhaps the managers could try to use a more consultative style. Simply by seeking the opinions of employees and showing that their input is valued, better relationships can be formed, which may lead to the development of a more positive culture.

In terms of **change management**, it has already been noted that **employee resistance** is one of the greatest restraining forces. A positive culture can overcome this and may prevent a state of organisational inertia from developing. The creation of a Learning Organisation (see below) is one way that this can be achieved.

5.2   Change management theories

5.2.1 Senge's Learning Organisation theory

Principles of Peter Senge's theory of the Learning Organisation

Peter Senge wrote the first edition of *The Fifth Discipline: The Art and Practice of the Learning Organization* in 1990. In it, he defined a **Learning Organisation** as follows:

> Learning organizations [are] organizations where people continually expand their capacity to create the results they truly desire, where new and expansive patterns of thinking are nurtured, where collective aspiration is set free, and where people are continually learning to see the whole together.
>
> Senge PM. (1990) *The Fifth Discipline: The Art and Practice of the Learning Organization*. Random House.

In this way, a business can transform with new ideas and a creative energy. Senge discusses the five disciplines that are necessary to generate a Learning Organisation. By 'discipline', he means theory and technique that must be studied and mastered to be put into practice.

Systems thinking

According to Senge, systems thinking is the fifth discipline:

> It is the discipline that integrates the disciplines, fusing them into a coherent body of theory and practice. It keeps them from being separate gimmicks or the latest organization change fads. Without a systemic orientation, there is no motivation to look at how the disciplines interrelate. By enhancing each of the other disciplines, it continually reminds us that the whole can exceed the sum of its parts.
>
> Senge PM. (1990) *The Fifth Discipline: The Art and Practice of the Learning Organization*. Random House.

Systems thinking relies on analysing the relationships that exist within an organisation. By doing this, and looking at the cause and effect of issues, the business can come up with long-term solutions rather than quick fixes. It is how managers can see the entire organisation, rather than small segments.

Personal mastery

This focus is on the individual employees in a business continuously self-improving:

> Personal mastery is the discipline of continually clarifying and deepening our personal vision, of focusing our energies, of developing patience and of seeing reality objectively.
>
> Senge PM. (1990) *The Fifth Discipline: The Art and Practice of the Learning Organization*. Random House.

Senge considers personal mastery to reflect developing proficiency in work and becoming committed to lifelong learning.

Mental models

According to Senge:

> These are deeply ingrained assumptions, generalizations or even pictures or images that influence how we understand the world and how we take action. Mental models of what can or cannot be done in different management settings are no less deeply entrenched. Many insights into new markets or outmoded organizational practices fail to get put into practice because they conflict with powerful, tacit mental models.
>
> Senge PM. (1990) *The Fifth Discipline: The Art and Practice of the Learning Organization*. Random House.

To generate a Learning Organisation, Senge believes that the mental models must be identified, and if they are detrimental to the ideals of a Learning Organisation or will restrain a change process, then they need to be replaced with mental models that will have the desired effect.

Building shared vision

Senge believes that there needs to be practices that transform an individual's vision into a shared vision that encourages people to develop a Learning Organisation.

> When there is a genuine vision (as opposed to the all-too-familiar 'vision statement'), people excel and learn, not because they are told to, but because they want to. But many leaders have personal visions that never get translated into shared visions that galvanize an organization.
>
> Senge PM. (1990) *The Fifth Discipline: The Art and Practice of the Learning Organization*. Random House.

Team learning

Team learning is an important discipline because it places emphasis on the team rather than the individual. The desired outcome of producing a Learning Organisation is more likely to be achieved if there is team learning.

> Team learning is vital because teams, not individuals, are the fundamental learning unit in modern organizations. Occasionally, in business, there are striking examples where the intelligence of the team exceeds the intelligence of the individuals in the team, and where teams develop extraordinary capacities for coordinated action. The discipline of team learning starts with 'dialogue', the capacity of members of a team to suspend assumptions and enter into a genuine 'thinking together'. When teams are truly learning, not only are they producing extraordinary results, but the individual members are growing more rapidly than could have occurred otherwise.
>
> Senge PM. (1990) *The Fifth Discipline: The Art and Practice of the Learning Organization*. Random House.

> **Hint**
>
> Learn more by reading Peter Senge's book *The Fifth Discipline: The Art and Practice of the Learning Organization*, Random House, 1990.

5.2.2 Lewin's Three-step Change Model

Lewin's **Three-step Change Model** was first published in 1947. It was one of the first theories that provided businesses with a process to follow when implementing change. By today's standards it might appear to be a little simplistic, but many of the change models that have been developed since have a basis in Lewin's model. Figure 5.1 provides an overview of the essence of the model.

Please note that Lewin called the last stage 'freezing', but it is mostly known as 'refreezing', as it reverts to a fixed state (although it is a fixed state that is different from what it was originally).

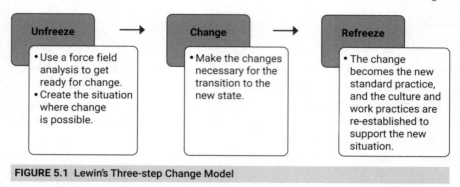

Unfreeze
- Use a force field analysis to get ready for change.
- Create the situation where change is possible.

Change
- Make the changes necessary for the transition to the new state.

Refreeze
- The change becomes the new standard practice, and the culture and work practices are re-established to support the new situation.

FIGURE 5.1 Lewin's Three-step Change Model

Unfreeze

This is removing inertia and preparing stakeholders for the change. It involves breaking down the old way of doing things. It reflects the stage in Lewin's Force Field Analysis theory where the driving forces have pushed through the restraining forces and have dominance.

Change

This is the process of transition. In this stage, new processes or practices may be introduced to the business. Effectively, the change is put in place. Some **support** systems may need to be implemented to assist with the smooth transition.

Refreeze

This is the establishment of a new stability and culture. This may require new policies to be introduced to reinforce the changed business so that it becomes the status quo. The culture should reflect the changed situation as well.

It is important to note that after completing the process of change, the business should not remain in the new state forever. As managers monitor their business's performance through KPIs, the need may arise for another change to be implemented. When this occurs, the change model can be used again for the new circumstances.

5.2.3 Low- and high-risk strategies to overcome employee resistance to change

Once the managers of a business have decided, after monitoring relevant KPIs, that change is necessary and they have thought about the process to follow, they need to consider the ways in which they can minimise the restraining forces, in particular, employee resistance.

Low-risk strategies

Low-risk strategies are methods of introducing change that are likely to be well accepted with little resistance. Here are some examples.

Communication

Managers need to communicate the changes clearly, making sure that all stakeholders are aware of the process that will be undertaken and the benefits that should result. Sometimes employees fear the unknown. When the details of changes are fully explained, they may find that it's not as bad as they feared and may be happy to support the changes.

Empowerment

One way to encourage employee support for a change is to involve them. If employees are **empowered** to make decisions and offer suggestions about the change process, then they are less likely to resist it.

Support

Managers also need to be aware of the fears and concerns that employees and other stakeholders may have regarding the change, and offer support. This may be in the form of training or simply encouragement.

Alternatively, the business can employ a 'change agent' or 'change enablement officer', who are consultants who specialise in the introduction of change. They would be employed to support the managers in an organisation for a period of time, leaving once the changes have been fully implemented. Sometimes change agents are existing staff members who are appointed to the role for the duration of the change process. The employment of a change agent can assist the managers of the business to select the best method of implementing change, taking into consideration situational variables such as:

- the urgency of the change (does the business have the luxury to spend a year on the process or must it occur within a couple of months?)
- the extent of the change (will the whole business be affected or just one branch or section?)
- the skill levels of both employees and managers (if the change requires retraining, the process may be more time-consuming and costly)
- the support from management and employees (it is obviously easier to implement change in a business where everyone is supportive of the change; when there is resistance, it is important that low-risk strategies are employed)
- the nature of the change (the process of implementation will be different if the change is to be the installation of a new computer system compared with a merger with another business).

Incentives

Sometimes it might be necessary to offer **incentives** to encourage employees or customers to embrace a change. Businesses often have introductory offers to get customers to try a new product. Employees might require some inducement to accept the change. This needs to be seen as encouragement, not a bribe to simply go along with the change without regard to their misgivings; it is something that employees would need to work towards.

High-risk strategies

High-risk strategies are methods of introducing change that are likely to be resisted by employees and other stakeholders. While they might be effective in the short term, they may have negative consequences in the long term.

Manipulation

In some circumstances, managers may resort to **manipulation** of information to push a change through. This might mean leaving out pertinent information or making the change sound more advantageous to the employees than it really is. This can also mean manipulating workers by offering bribes to get them to just accept the change.

Threats

In extreme cases, managers may **threaten** workers' job security or their prospects of getting promotions in order to implement change. It can be a case of 'go along with the change or find another job'.

Neither of these high-risk strategies is a desirable method of change management as they can create distrust, lower morale and damage the corporate culture. They can also create further problems as workers are less likely to conform to the changes if they feel that they have been forced on them.

5.3 Considerations after implementing change

5.3.1 Effect of change on stakeholders

Whatever the change is, it will impact a number of stakeholders. Obviously the impact will differ based on a wide range of factors, including the nature of the actual change.

So, to illustrate this concept, consider the following scenario: Nouk's is a large privately-owned department store. The **owners** and managers have reviewed their KPIs and they decide that they can no longer afford to keep their shops open in regional cities such as Bendigo and Geelong. While online sales are booming, and customers are still buying in the shops in the capital cities, the cost of keeping the regional shops open is becoming prohibitive.

The following effects could occur.

- Owners: If Nouk's has been a family business for a long time, then there is not just the financial impact, but also the impact to them personally as they feel responsible for the closure and lack of employment in Bendigo and Geelong.
- Managers: The managers of the regional shops will face redundancy. The human resource manager of Nouk's will need to organise this process for all employees who will lose their jobs.
- Employees: The employees of the regional stores will also face redundancy.
- Customers: Customers of the regional shops will now have to shop online or travel to the capital city if they still want to purchase items from Nouk's.
- **Suppliers**: The amount of stock required from suppliers will be reduced as the regional shops close. There may have been some items that were only available in the regional shops. Those suppliers may have now lost a big customer.
- The general **community**: With many people losing their jobs in the regional cities, the lower incomes may be felt throughout their entire community. Perhaps these people can no longer afford to eat out at restaurants or they may postpone buying new furniture or cars. People employed at those businesses may also find that they face the possibility of being made redundant if sales fall drastically.

5.3.2 Corporate social responsibility considerations

Whatever change is initiated, managers would still need to be mindful of the business's own policies on social responsibility and community expectations regarding ethical behaviour (**corporate social responsibility**). For example, if the managers of a business decide that they are going to implement new machinery, they would need to make sure that the machinery is sourced from a company that treats its own employees ethically, that the machinery will not pollute the environment and that any changes to the internal environment of the organisation are handled in an ethical and socially responsible manner. This could mean keeping the staff informed about the changes, especially if some of them will be retrenched or redeployed as a result of this change.

5.3.3 Review to determine effectiveness of change

Once the change has been implemented and the structures and support policies are in place so that it becomes the new standard, the work of managers is still not quite finished. Some clearly identifiable goals would have been set at the start of the process. There would have been no point in introducing a change if the managers were not trying to achieve something. This 'something' is usually related to better results in their selected KPIs. For example, if managers of a supermarket wanted to increase their market share by 10%, then after a period of time has lapsed to give the change time to have the desired effect, managers would revisit the KPI to see if market share has increased. If there has been no significant improvement, then it is clear that the transformation process has not been successful. A review of the **effectiveness** of the process could be undertaken with the aim of more success in any future endeavours. Without a review, it may not be apparent that the business is pouring money into ineffective strategies. Continued success requires constant monitoring of KPIs.

CHAPTER 5

Glossary

capital resources Manufactured goods used in production.

change management Controlling the introduction of alterations to a business.

communication A two-way process of effectively sending and receiving information.

community A group of people who live near each other or have something in common.

corporate culture The shared values, beliefs and behaviours of the people in an organisation.

corporate social responsibility (CSR) Where businesses take responsibility for their actions that impact on the wider community through the use of ethical practices.

customers Those who purchase goods and/or services from a business.

effectiveness The process of achieving all stated goals and objectives.

employee A worker in a business who is paid an income in exchange for their labour.

employee resistance A state that occurs when the workers in a business fight or block a change that is being introduced.

empowerment Giving employees permission to make limited decisions without having to consult superiors.

high-risk strategies Methods of introducing change that are likely to be resisted by employees and other stakeholders.

incentives Things that can be provided or offered to encourage or motivate someone.

innovation The development of something new, either a product or a production technique.

inputs The resources necessary to make the product.

key performance indicators (KPIs) Criteria that can be used to evaluate the success and achievements of an organisation.

labour resources The people and roles required to produce the good and/or service.

leadership The ability to influence and inspire workers so that they want to achieve organisational objectives.

lean production The establishment of systems that will eliminate waste and inefficiencies of any kind in the process of making a good or providing a service.

A+ DIGITAL FLASHCARDS
Revise this topic's key terms and concepts by scanning the QR code or typing the URL into your browser.

https://get.ga/aplus-vce-busmgmt-u34

Learning Organisation Organisations where employees are encouraged to work in teams with a shared vision to continually learn.

low-risk strategies Methods of introducing change that are likely to be well accepted with little resistance.

managers Those in leadership positions who have responsibility for a section of a business.

management skills The abilities that benefit managers to perform their roles.

management style The preferred method of operating as a manager, including ways of making decisions and inclusiveness of employees.

manipulation Changing information in order to provide an altered message that persuades someone to a different point of view.

natural resources Things that come from the land and are used in the production process.

outsourcing The process of hiring another business or consultant to complete a task or project.

owners People who have bought and/or established their own businesses.

quality A standard that meets the needs and/or wants of the customer.

strategies Practices or actions implemented with the aim of achieving a particular effect.

suppliers Those who provide the goods and/or services that are required by other businesses.

support Assistance to help an employee to perform better.

technology The application of science resulting in machinery and devices.

threat A stated intention to do harm or prevent career progression.

Three-step Change Model A process (unfreeze, change, refreeze) to introduce change in a business.

training A short-term process aimed at improving technical skill levels.

Revision summary

The first column in the table below has the key knowledge points of Unit 4 Area of Study 2. Read the suggestions in the second column for ways that you can complete notes that will be useful for preparation for both School-assessed Coursework tasks as well as your end-of-year exam.

Unit 4 Area of Study 2 Implementing Change	Suggestions for summary notes
The importance of leadership in change management	Explain how effective leadership can benefit the change process. It can be helpful to turn this around to state how change implementation would be more difficult without effective change.
Management strategies to respond to key performance indicators and/or seek new business opportunities, including staff training, staff motivation, change in management styles or management skills, increased investment in technology, improving quality in production, cost cutting, initiating lean production techniques and redeployment of resources (natural, labour and capital), innovation, global sourcing of inputs, overseas manufacture and global outsourcing	For each of these, explain how it can assist a business in addressing poor performance as reflected in one specific KPI. Use your class notes and/or the table on pages 80 and 81 of *A+ VCE Business Management Study Notes* to assist you. When you get to the redeployment of resources (natural, labour and capital) begin with definitions and examples of natural, capital and labour resources.
Corporate culture and strategies for its development	Make sure that you can suggest a few different ways to develop corporate culture (see the notes in this chapter). You must also be able to state how Senge's theory can be used to create a positive culture for change.
An overview of the principles of the Learning Organisation (Senge) and the need to create a positive culture for change	Students tend to find this theory difficult, so carefully follow the steps below. First explain what a Learning Organisation is. Now write about the five disciplines. For each one, explain what it is and state how it can assist a business that is going through the process of change. • personal mastery • mental models • building shared vision • team learning • systems thinking. Finally, re-read Section 5.2.1 to see how a Learning Organisation can provide a positive culture for change. This is most important because it explains why it is included in the area of study that is about implementing change.
Low-risk strategies to overcome employee resistance including communication, empowerment, support and incentives	Define 'low-risk strategies'. Now explain how each of the strategies can overcome employee resistance to change. Define 'empowerment' in your response here as well. Make sure that you discuss incentives, in terms of being offered a benefit in response to successful change. It must be seen to be quite different from a bribe, which is not related to performance.

»

CHAPTER 5 – REVISION SUMMARY

›› High-risk strategies to overcome employee resistance including manipulation and threat	Define 'high-risk strategy'. This is a little different from the low-risk strategies. For each of these, explain how it can be used effectively to overcome employee resistance to change, but also add why it is considered high risk to use each of these strategies.
Key principles of the Three-step Change Model (Lewin)	Explain each of the three steps of Lewin's change model. In your response, apply the three steps to a change example from a real business that you studied.
The effect of change on stakeholder groups including owners, managers, employees, customers, suppliers and the general community	State the effect of a real business change that you studied on each of these stakeholders. Be really specific. Which employees do you mean? Those working in the IT section of the business? Those in sales? Suppliers of what exactly? Which 'general' community?
Corporate social responsibility considerations when implementing change	First explain why businesses need to consider corporate social responsibility when making changes. Now provide a couple of examples of the things that managers might consider to ensure that they are demonstrating it when making changes. Use real business examples here.
The importance of reviewing key performance indicators to evaluate the effectiveness of business transformation	One way to revise this in note form is to state what could happen if managers didn't use KPIs to evaluate the effectiveness of business transformation. What could go wrong? That will tell you why it is important to do it.

VCE Business Management Study Design 2023–2027 p. 23, © VCAA 2022

Congratulations – you have now revised the entire course!

Exam practice

Solutions for this section start on page 114.

Question 1 (2 marks) ◼◼◻

Explain how effective leadership can assist in the implementation of change.

Question 2 (2 + 2 = 4 marks) ◼◼◻

Explain how the strategy of changing a management style can assist a business in improving two different KPIs.

Question 3 (2 + 2 = 4 marks marks) ◼◼◻

Outline two different strategies that a coffee shop could implement to increase profit.

Question 4 (2 marks) ◼◼◻

Explain how a business could access new opportunities within Australia.

Question 5 (1 mark) ◼◻◻

Describe the role of Austrade.

Question 6 (2 marks) ◼◼◻

What is a Learning Organisation?

Question 7 (2 marks) ◼◼◻

Why is systems thinking considered to be the fifth discipline?

Question 8 (3 marks) ◼◻◻

Outline the steps in Lewin's change model.

Question 9 (1 marks) ◼◻◻

Which stage of Lewin's change model relates to his Force Field Analysis theory?

Question 10 (2 marks) ◼◼◻

Explain whether the owner or manager of a business should still monitor KPIs and consider further changes, even if the initial change process has been completed.

Question 11 (1 mark) ◼◻◻

Define 'low-risk strategy' in relation to introducing change.

Question 12 (2 marks) ◼◼◻

Describe two ways that managers could use low-risk strategies to overcome employee resistance when introducing a change.

Question 13 (1 mark) ◼◼◻

Explain how manipulation can be a high-risk strategy.

Question 14 (2 marks) ◼◼◻

Why is it best to avoid using high-risk strategies when implementing change?

Question 15 (2 marks) ◼◼◻

Explain why managers need to evaluate the effectiveness of the business transformation.

Question 16 (6 marks)

As explained in the following case study, Shandra's Dairy Ltd wants to diversify into the snack food market within the next three years. Apply Lewin's Three-step Change Model to assist Shandra's Dairy Ltd with this future goal.

CASE STUDY

The following is the first page from the 2017 'Report to Shareholders' of Shandra's Dairy Ltd.

Commencing as a family-run business 15 years ago, we are now one of the largest independent dairies in Australia. We are proud of the fact that our raw materials are sourced from local suppliers and that customer satisfaction remains at the centre of our operations. We use a strict quality control strategy to maintain the overall excellence of our products.

Business highlights in 2017

- Market share increased from 15% to 17%
- Increase in volumes of sales to over 10 million litres of ice-cream
- Installation of four modern wind turbines at a total cost of $1.25 million, reducing carbon emissions by 3500 tonnes per year, thus assisting us in meeting our 2020 renewable energy target
- A saving of $500 000 per year on electricity bills due to the installation of 600 solar panels

One of our key objectives is to enhance levels of environmental sustainability and make our entire site self-sufficient through renewable energy. Our CEO, Johanna Taylor, is eager to ensure that over 23% of the electricity used comes from renewable sources by 2020. This fits in with the Australian Government's Renewable Energy Target.

'Our commitment to renewable energy has meant an increase in expenses and debt in the short term, but shareholders will continue to see value as the saving in electricity costs will be sustained into the future.'

— Johanna Taylor

Another objective is to become a truly global brand – to do this we need to diversify. Our aim is to launch into the snack food market, concentrating on potato chips. These can be produced at our present manufacturing plant and with the use of our existing suppliers. We believe that this could commence by 2020 and we could export to markets in over 20 countries.

Future goals

- Implement a second strategy to improve quality by 1 July 2018
- Diversify into the snack food market within the next three years

---

Question 17 (3 marks)

Dennis Greeves is the manager of a highly successful, Melbourne-based burger chain. In response to a decline in sales and a change in customer tastes, Dennis has made the decision to implement a policy of using only ethically sourced, high-quality local ingredients. Dennis is aware that a new pricing strategy will be required as a result and that the Executive Chef will require support to implement the changes.

Explain how Dennis could use the low-risk strategy of support to overcome possible employee resistance to the changes.

Question 18 (4 marks) ©VCAA 2019 SA Q5d ●●

Apply the principles of **two** steps from the Three-step Change Model (Lewin) to Dennis' decision to implement a new pricing strategy to address the decline in sales.

Question 19 (6 marks) ©VCAA 2020 SA Q6 ●●●

Analyse how societal attitudes have been a driving force for change in a contemporary business that you have studied this year.

Question 20 (4 marks) ©VCAA 2020 SB Q6 ●●○

Based on the following case study, outline how two of the restraining forces in business listed below might influence Manitta Mining's ability to successfully introduce change to business operations in the future:

- organisational inertia
- legislation
- financial considerations
- employees.

CASE STUDY

Below is an extract of a speech delivered to the shareholders of Manitta Mining by its Chief Executive Officer at its annual general meeting on 7 August 2020.

Our business faces significant challenges. Staff turnover has increased significantly over a five-year period. The business's share price on the Australian Securities Exchange (ASX) has decreased by 15% over the same five-year period. Sales are also down and the company has struggled to reduce the number of workplace accidents in our mines.

As Chief Executive Officer of Manitta Mining for more than 15 years, I am pleased to tell you the long-term outlook for the company remains strong. Since the appointment of a new operations manager, Dr Margaret Sherckle, in February 2020, the number of workplace accidents has decreased by 25%. The number of workplace accidents is a very important key performance indicator (KPI) for the business and a key business objective is to improve workplace safety.

Manitta Mining currently has more than 20 000 employees, each of whom I consider to be part of the 'Manitta family'. While business efficiency and effectiveness are important, the goal of ensuring that our employees return home safely each day is our priority.

A safe workplace will reduce staff turnover. It will also reduce staff absenteeism. We aim to keep staff turnover below 5% in the year ahead. This will reduce associated costs. For example, reduced staff turnover will reduce staff training costs. WorkCover premiums will also fall. Manitta Mining expects that increased employee retention will lead to significant increases in the rate of productivity growth during the next 12 months.

Finally, I would like to thank you, the shareholders. Loyalty deserves to be rewarded. The implementation of strategies that improve business performance through increased productivity growth will ensure that your investment grows in turn.

Thank you.

Exam practice: Case study

Solutions for this section start on page 116.

Coop's Mobile Homes (CMH) is a medium-sized business that manufactures retro-style caravans. While retro in appearance, the vans are fitted with modern fixtures and the latest technology. There are 110 employees in the Victorian manufacturing facility, with a further 60 employed in sales branches throughout Australia.

Blair Coop took over the running of the company from his father, Joe, in 2010.

KPI	Change over the past year
Net profit	↑ 2%
Staff turnover	0%
Level of waste	↑ 15%
Rate of staff absenteeism	↑ 30%

Blair has decided that he wants to pursue markets in the United States and Canada, but he has concerns about the absenteeism rates and the level of waste.

Shutterstock.com/design us studio

Questions

Use the case study provided to answer the questions in this section.

Question 1 (2 marks)

Explain why leadership is important when a business is undergoing change.

Question 2 (12 marks)

Propose a different management strategy that responds to each key performance indicator in the table and explain how it could assist CMH.

Question 3 (2 marks)

Outline one strategy that Blair could implement that would assist in his objective to seek a global market.

Question 4 (4 marks)

Explain the key principles of Senge's Learning Organisation.

Question 5 (6 marks) ●●

Blair decides to confront the high levels of absenteeism, but is faced with employee resistance. Discuss whether the high-risk strategy of threat or the low-risk strategy of support is more likely to be effective in this situation.

Question 6 (9 marks) ●●

Apply Lewin's Three-step Change Model to the decision to pursue overseas markets for sales of the CMH retro caravans.

Question 7 (6 marks) ●●

Explain the possible impact on three different stakeholders of CMH if Blair goes ahead with the change to become an exporter of caravans.

Question 8 (4 marks) ●●

Discuss the issues of corporate social responsibility that Blair Coop must consider if the company is to become an exporter of caravans.

Question 9 (5 marks) ●●

A year has now passed since Blair changed from being a purely domestic supplier of caravans to becoming an exporter. Using the data in the case study, explain why it is important to evaluate the effectiveness of the transformation of CMH.

Total = 50 marks

SOLUTIONS

UNIT 3: MANAGING A BUSINESS

Chapter 1 Area of Study 1

Exam practice solutions

1 There are several possible answers to the question. Here are some examples.

- Advantages of establishing a partnership
  - The workload is shared by the partners, rather than borne by one person.
  - There is a wider range of ideas to contribute to decision-making, rather than the sole trader having to source all ideas by themselves.
  - There are more sources of capital to set up the business, rather than the sole trader having to come up with all the required funds.
- Disadvantages of setting up a partnership
  - There may be disputes if the partners have different ideas on the direction of the business, whereas a sole trader can pursue whatever course they want.
  - Profits have to be split between the partners, whereas a sole trader keeps all profits.

2 Social enterprises sell goods and services to earn an income and profit that can be put towards a social cause such as reducing poverty or environmental issues.

3 • Private companies are not listed on the stock exchange, whereas public companies are.
  - Private companies cannot have more than 50 shareholders, whereas public companies can have any number of shareholders.

4 • The owner of the hairdressing salon is interested in the profitability of the business because they earn their income from the profits that the business generates.
  - Customers have an interest because once they find a hairdressing salon that they like, they would want it to continue operating and providing a consistent quality of service.

> There are many possible answers to the question. Here is a list of some of the stakeholders that you may have written about in your answer:
> - suppliers of hairdressing products
> - other hairdressers in the same town/suburb (the competitors)
> - employees of the salon (hairdressers).

5 This statement is false. There is an expectation that all businesses will demonstrate corporate social responsibility. This is a reflection of changing societal attitudes and values. Whether it is a large bank operating ethically when dealing with millions of dollars of customers' money, or the local coffee shop using fair-trade coffee, customers' expectations will be shown through their buying or investment behaviours.

6 a Because workers will be directly affected by the roster, it makes sense to include them in the decision-making process; hence, participative might be the best style to use. (Consultative would also be acceptable.) If the workers have some say in the rosters, they are more likely to accept them, increasing morale levels and productivity.

   b This is a senior-level plan; therefore, the final decisions should rest with the managers. Suitable styles would include consultative (especially if employees could make valuable suggestions) or persuasive. While the autocratic style would probably work, it would not be the best as stakeholders, especially employees, should be informed about the reasons for the change to the business.

7 Laissez-faire is not a suitable style in most businesses because there is a lack of control. Without control measures in place, businesses run the risk of inefficient resource use leading to reduced productivity. Employees may not exhibit the required behaviours and may take the business into directions that conflict with broad organisational objectives.

8 A manager with interpersonal skills has the ability to empathise and interact positively with employees, while a manager with good communication skills has the ability to send and receive information clearly. Managers could be very effective communicators, while having poor interpersonal skills. Their ability as leaders would be lessened, however.

9 Managers using the consultative management style will gather information, suggestions and feedback from stakeholders, but they make the final decision alone. If they did not have good decision-making skills, they would find this difficult and may be forced to adopt another style that is less appropriate for the situation.

10 While there is some truth in this statement, it is not totally correct. Managers in businesses today recognise the importance of employees and understand that if the employees remain motivated with high levels of morale, then they will be productive and loyal. The autocratic management style can tend to alienate workers as they are simply issued with instructions. For this reason, most businesses will tend to use a management style that shows more consideration for the employees and their thoughts.

11 The official culture is what is stated in the company motto or mission statement, while the real culture reflects how things actually operate in terms of shared values, beliefs and behaviours of employees.

12 • If a business has a positive corporate culture, it is more likely that staff absenteeism rates will be low as employees will enjoy coming to work.

   • Productivity rates should remain high. A positive culture reflects a workplace where employees are satisfied with their conditions and are motivated, which leads to high levels of productivity.

13 An external focus means that employees want to delight customers, beat competitors and care for their communities. These are all positive attributes for a business. If employees have an external focus, it will provide the basis for a positive corporate culture as they work together with common goals that will benefit the business.

14 If managers recruit new employees with the desired attitudes, skills, values and personalities, then they are likely to support the official culture and the real culture will tend to reflect this through their actions. If, however, new employees come into a workplace where the culture is toxic with poor work habits and low morale levels, there is a possibility that they may succumb to the negative culture that surrounds them.

> A question that asks you to 'discuss' requires consideration of strengths/weaknesses, pros/cons, advantages/disadvantages; more than one point of view should be considered.

15 Given that there are many benefits from having a positive corporate culture, it matters equally to a large or a small business. There can be a danger in a small business, where everyone knows each other well, that employees could lapse into unprofessional or poor work habits. For this reason, the culture needs to be positive to generate high morale levels and to reduce the staff turnover rate. This is a common goal that applies to both large and small businesses.

16 Sample answer: A business may choose to operate as a partnership rather than a sole trader so that it can benefit from the extra factors that partnerships provide such as additional start-up capital from each partner as well as the expertise that each partner brings to the business. (2 marks)

> This question is worth 2 marks, so ensure that you do more than simply state a reason. Also note that definitions are not required unless explicitly stated.

17 Sample answer: A partnership is a business structure where up to 20 people own and run a business together. Many doctors' surgeries are partnerships between a number of doctors. (2 marks)

> Make sure you give the assessors enough information to be able to award two marks, not just one.

18 Sample answer: Employees are the people who work for a business to allow it to achieve its objectives. Their interests often include security in their job and increasing their remuneration through pay rises and bonuses. They will also often value opportunities for development and advancement. Managers are the people in charge of sections of the business. They are responsible for business success, thus their main interest is achieving business objectives. They will also have personal interests including opportunities for advancement and praise for their work. Ocean Hub may see a conflict between these stakeholders due to the financial interests of each.

As managers will want to see more profit going towards fulfilling their social objective, employees may be unlikely to see pay rises or bonuses. Alternatively, if employees do receive more remuneration, less funds will be accessible to fund Ocean Hub's new classes, and thus its social objective will not be achieved to the same extent.

Additionally, their personal interests may conflict. Managers seeking praise for their work during Ocean Hub's expansion may avoid delegating tasks, thus not allowing for employees to develop their skills and feel they are contributing. On the other hand, allowing employees to contribute may result in managers being shown up. This may limit their chance for recognition. (5 marks)

VCAA 2018 SB Q5 VCE Business Management examination report

> In order to answer this question well, the selection of two stakeholders who could, potentially, be in conflict is vital.

19 Sample answer: A business objective is a goal which an organisation sets out to achieve in a given time period. A business objective may include to 'increase profit' or to 'fulfil a social need'. (2 marks)

VCAA 2020 SA Q1a VCE Business Management examination report

> While this is a straightforward question, you need to ensure that you have enough information in your answer to be awarded two marks.

20 Sample answer: An autocratic style refers to when management have centralised decision-making and communication authorities. Most commonly managers provide employees with clear directions to complete a task, and regularly check in on employee performance. An advantage of John using this style is that he is able to make quick decisions in his bakery, since decision-making is centralised. This will mean that less time is spent making a decision, leading to less time of a low productivity. If productivity isn't affected, John's more likely to achieve his objective of increasing net profit by 10%. Another advantage of this style is that John can provide his employees with clear directives to complete a task, meaning that employees will know how to complete a task with higher competence, since they won't be confused (because of clear directions).

However, a disadvantage of this style is that John's employees will experience a low morale, since they are delegated tasks, and have no inputs at John's Bakery. This may lead to staff continuing to be absent, decreasing the likeliness of the bakery achieving objectives. Another disadvantage is that this style doesn't allow for a large pool of ideas from employees, as the manager makes decisions with no input. This may result in a lower quality decision being made if John is using his ideas/creativity when making a decision.

Overall, John should not utilise the autocratic style because employees will experience a low morale as they do not provide any input, leading to most feeling underappreciated. This is because staff feeling like this are more likely to work at a lower productivity, resulting in the objectives of the bakery not being met. (5 marks)

VCAA 2020 SA Q1b VCE Business Management examination report

> This is quite a tricky question as you need to evaluate, not just discuss. It's also important that you don't suggest other styles of management – the question did not ask for that.

Exam practice: Case study solutions

> **Note**
> The answers provided for the case study are model answers. They are not necessarily the only correct answers to the questions. Students should check with their teachers to see if their answers would be considered correct.

1 Market share refers to the percentage of sales or business of one firm, compared with its competitors in the same industry. Supermarkets in Australia compete for market share, with Coles and Woolworths having the biggest shares and smaller competitors such as Aldi and IGA having smaller shares of the market. (2 marks)

2 Sole traders are able to make their own decisions about such things as their opening hours and the menus. They also get to keep all profits. Partnerships, however, have the benefits of sharing the workload. In the case of a 7-day-a-week operation, it means that the partners can arrange to have some time off each week. Sole traders would also find it difficult to take time off to have a holiday or break from the business unless they have an employee that they trust to run the café in their absence. Partners can arrange separate times to take leave from their business. While there might be some disputes about the priorities of the café, if the partners have a good working relationship, running a café that is open every day might be more manageable for a partnership than it would be for a sole trader. (4 marks)

3 The suppliers of products such as bread and meat are stakeholders of Frost. Stakeholders are those who have an interest in an organisation, or those who could be affected by decisions made by the business. The food suppliers' interests are to receive a maximum amount of money from Frost in exchange for their products.

Frost's customers are another stakeholder. They would want high-quality food for a reasonable price. Given that there is competition in the town, if the price is too high, they may go to the other café. The customers would not want the café owners to pay excessive amounts for the food supplies because this would have to be reflected in the prices that they set for their food. This presents a conflicting interest between the suppliers and the customers of Frost. (4 marks)

4 Consultative managers seek feedback about matters before they make a decision. The final decision is theirs. Kathryn would need to have good decision-making skills to be an effective consultative manager. Decision-making is the ability to select the best course of action from a range of options. Kathryn would be doing that if she were a consultative manager because she would seek information from customers, employees or industry bodies to learn what her options are. From this she can make the final decision alone. (2 marks)

5 An autocratic manager is one who does not seek input, but makes decisions on their own and tells employees what they need to do. Anne is an autocratic manager at Frost. This can be effective because employees know exactly what they are meant to do. They do not have to make decisions for themselves. If the employees are just there to earn some cash without seeing the job as a career pathway, this can be appropriate. Tony, on the other hand, is a participative manager at Frost. He believes that the involvement of employees in decision-making is important. This is a more time-consuming process and can be good to raise the morale levels of employees because they feel that their input is valued.

Having one of each style of manager could, however, just lead to confusion for the employees. Depending on which manager is present on the day, the expectations for employees could be vastly different. This could result in jobs not being done, or being done in ways that the managers don't like, hence reducing the chance of achieving the business's objectives. This is clearly not an effective way to run a business. (6 marks)

6 Corporate culture refers to the shared values, beliefs and behaviours of the people in an organisation. It is important for a café because the employees deal with the public directly. If the culture is negative and it is apparent that the employees dislike their work, don't communicate well and demonstrate apathy, then this will be reflected in their work and felt by the customers who may choose to go to a competitor's café where there is a more positive culture and atmosphere. (2 marks)

Total = 20 marks

Chapter 2 Area of Study 2

Exam practice solutions

1 Motivated employees are more likely to be productive while at work. The high productivity rates can lead to more goods being produced, more sales happening or more services being provided for customers, all of which can give the business a competitive edge.

2 Maslow's theory of needs is considered to be a hierarchy because there is a developmental order – one level must be achieved or satisfied before a person is able to move on to the next.

3 Goals need to be specific so that the information is clear, allowing less room for error and individual interpretation. Goals need to be challenging or difficult because people tend to exert more effort and try harder to attain more difficult goals. Of course, the goals should be set so that they are achievable, so they also need to be realistic.

4 • The drive to acquire: Managers could satisfy this drive through a decent remuneration package for the employee.

  • The drive to bond: Managers could satisfy this drive through placing employees in supportive teams to conduct their work.

  • The drive to learn: Managers could satisfy this drive by sending employees out to attend a course to develop new skills that would be useful in their jobs.

  • The drive to defend: As this drive is not activated until there is a threat, managers could ensure that employees don't feel that their jobs are at risk, through positive feedback or meaningful performance appraisals.

5 One advantage of using performance-related pay is that employees who have financial commitments such as mortgages or families to support are likely to appreciate the extra money and will be motivated to work hard to receive it.

  One disadvantage of using performance-related pay is that not everyone is motivated by money. If the job is boring or the relationships between employees and managers at the workplace are breaking down, then it is likely that other motivational strategies that focus on the employees' intrinsic needs would be more beneficial.

6 On-the-job training refers to the development of skills that occurs at the workplace, usually during normal working hours, whereas off-the-job training refers to the development of skills that occurs away from the workplace, often involving courses.

7 Two advantages of on-the-job training are that it can be conducted during normal working hours and that money does not have to be spent on expensive courses. Two advantages of off-the-job training are that it is conducted away from the distractions of work and that expert training providers can be used.

8 Performance appraisals are conducted to evaluate how well an employee is doing their work. They can be used to identify areas in which the employee needs to improve their skills and/or knowledge and can also be used as a forum to recognise the good work that is being performed.

9 Management by objectives (MBO) may be used to manage employees' performances. MBO involves setting clear objectives that are reviewed as part of a process to evaluate employee performance. A second strategy is self-evaluation. This involves employees documenting their achievements and deciding whether they have the required training. It is part of performance management as it allows managers to suggest learning strategies to enhance the employees' skills and/or knowledge.

10 Redundancies are similar to resignation in that employees leave the organisation. The employees have not done anything wrong in both cases. They are different, however, in terms of who makes the decision. With a resignation, the employee has decided that they no longer wish to work at the business. With redundancy, the managers have determined that there is no longer a position for the employee, usually due to a downturn in sales or profit.

A 'compare' question requires both similarities and differences to be stated.

11 Unions and employer associations are similar in the way that they both look after the interests of groups in terms of their legal positions. They offer support and advice. They are different, however, because while unions look out for the interests of employees, employer associations look out for the interests of the employers, which are usually businesses.

12 One strength of offering award pay and conditions is that employees will be given the minimum wages and conditions. This can keep costs low for a business.

One weakness of offering award pay and conditions is that because it is the minimum, it may not be enough to attract highly skilled workers, especially if competitors are offering agreements that contain higher pay rates.

13 Mediation is the process of getting an objective third party to try to assist two parties to resolve a dispute, whereas arbitration is the process whereby a third party makes a binding decision to resolve a dispute.

14 Protected action refers to industrial action, such as going on strike, that has been permitted to occur by the Fair Work Commission. It requires notice to be given to the employer about the type and duration of the action and can only occur during the period of negotiating a new agreement.

15 Any of the following would be correct.

- Human resource managers are often involved as employer representatives in the process of negotiating new agreements.

- Human resource managers are responsible for making sure that new or revised agreements are implemented correctly.

- Human resource managers may be required to negotiate in times of industrial unrest and disputes.

16 Sample answer: Car Bright should use on-the-job training. This is where employees improve their skills and knowledge while at the workplace, often while performing their actual job. Using on-the-job training will allow for Aaron's employees to improve their car cleaning services more effectively as they are able to learn with the actual equipment that they need to use. Furthermore, this will likely be more cost-effective for Aaron to implement rather than sending employees elsewhere for training. On-the-job training will result in highly skilled employees at Car Bright in this manner. However, this form of training can result in poor habits from trainers within the workplace being passed down to employees as it often relies on employees to teach other employees. Furthermore, there may be workplace interruptions which interfere with the learning of Car Bright's employees at the workplace. (4 marks)

VCAA 2017 SA Q3b VCE Business Management examination report

'Discuss' questions require looking at two sides of an option – pros and cons, benefits and limitations and so on. In order to get full marks, students would need to do this as well as applying the option to the situation at Car Bright.

17 Sample answer: Mediation is the process of getting an objective third party to try to assist two parties to resolve a dispute, whereas arbitration is the process whereby a third party makes a binding decision to resolve a dispute. They differ in that arbitration provides a resolution, whereas mediation relies on the parties working together to resolve the difference with the aid of a third party. (3 marks)

VCAA 2017 SA Q2 VCE Business Management examination report

18 Sample answer: Maslow's Hierarchy of Needs is a motivational theory that suggests there are five needs for employees in a business, and that once one need has been achieved it becomes obsolete as a motivating factor. Level of staff turnover is a measure of the number of employees who leave the business and are replaced within a given period of time.

The first need is physiological, as Mary should provide her employees with basic pay and wages; however, this likely will not help to reduce staff turnover as it is an expected entitlement.

The second need is safety, which involves Mary ensuring she follows OH&S [occupational health and safety] laws and ensures the staff at the childcare centre aren't in danger working in an environment where they may hurt themselves.

The third need is belonging, as Mary should attempt to create a sense of community between the staff and parents of the kids at the Childcare Centre, so the staff feel supported and loved and are less likely to leave the business.

The fourth need is self-esteem as the staff could be offered performance-related pay or a bonus by Mary, if they contribute extra to 123 Childcare Centre, by giving extra time to create activities for the children. As a result, staff turnover may decrease because the childcare workers feel as though their extra efforts are being recognised and rewarded.

The final need is self-actualisation, where the child carers have a desire to be challenged at work, and may be given an increased level of responsibility in being asked to plan a class or trip for the kids. As a result, Mary may see a decrease in staff turnover because the childcare workers feel as though they are working to their full potential at 123 Childcare, and are less likely to leave the business. (6 marks)

VCAA 2018 SA Q1c VCE Business Management examination report

A six-mark question such as this requires students to be able to demonstrate knowledge of all the levels of Maslow's Hierarchy of Needs; however, not all steps need to be applied to the situation at 123 Childcare Centre as they have been in the sample response.

19 Sample answer: Lawrence and Nohria's Four Drive Theory states that humans have four main drives that shape the way humans think and behave. These four drives include the drive to acquire (status and money), the drive to bond (social relationships), the drive to learn (develop abilities) and the drive to defend (defend themselves and the business).

In 2017 DeEll Bakery was exposed for underpaying employees. This theory could be applied to re-motivate staff. The drive to acquire could be satisfied by providing pay through an agreement that allows employees to acquire material items. The drive to bond could be applied through managers holding regular social gatherings where employees mingle with each other and build rapport.

DeEll Bakery could satisfy the drive to learn by offering training programs that can satisfy the curiosity and improve product knowledge and customer service skills. The drive to defend could be satisfied by ensuring DeEll Bakery has grievance procedures in place that everyone is aware of to be used when the need to defend arises.

Motivation strategies that DeEll Bakery could use is support; emotional/physical guidance provided to employees. This could be used to manage their employees as it will help to develop a positive corporate culture if employees see each other being supported. It will also help DeEll Bakery employees feel valued by the business and that managers greatly appreciate their contribution towards business objectives. (6 marks)

(Note: The business's name in this sample answer has been changed.)

VCAA 2019 SA Q6 VCE Business Management examination report

There is a lot to do in this question for six marks.
- Select a contemporary business case study.
- Link (apply) one motivational theory; select from the Hierarchy of Needs (Maslow), the Goal Setting Theory (Locke and Latham) or the Four Drive Theory (Lawrence and Nohria).
- Apply a motivational strategy (select from performance-related pay, career advancement, investment in training, support or sanction.)

20 Sample answer: Motivation refers to the level of energy, creativity and commitment one brings when performing a task. As employees are vital stakeholders in the achievement of business objectives, ensuring they remain motivated at work is crucial for both individual and business success and sustainability.

One motivation strategy is performance-related pay. This involves a financial reward being given to employees whose work has reached or exceeded a set standard. It may be in the form of bonuses or sales commissions. This extrinsic motivation acts to motivate many employees driven by money and driven to acquire material goods and possessions. This can act to improve their productivity at work, as they work more efficiently, knowing such reinforcement is available for admirable performance. This allows a business to achieve its objectives as employees strive to have their achievement recognised, working hard to generate a higher quality product or provide better customer service, both of which can improve customer satisfaction, sales and thus a business's profit due to increased revenue. However, this strategy can create a competitive culture within the business. This can lead to resentment and disputes as some employees feel overlooked and their contributions to the business unrecognised. It can also be a significant cost to a business due to the provision of money, increasing their expenses. Thus this strategy can enhance performance/motivation for some, but should not be the only option to employees. It can be largely unsustainable, and thus more effective for short term motivation. This is because employees will strive to reach the bonus or have their wage increased, and once achieved, are likely to revert to their prior performance and overall not remain motivated once acquired. Therefore, this provides short-term motivation for employees.

Another motivation strategy is investment in training, which acts to increase skills and knowledge of employees so they are better able to perform their jobs. By investing in training, such as on-the-job training including role modelling or mentoring, or off the job, whereby a business pays for an external course provider in the form of a lecture or conference, employees will feel valued and satisfied within a business. Such job satisfaction will increase their willingness to work hard to achieve business objectives, improving their productivity due to their motivation and engagement. It also allows them to develop a wider breadth of skills, to produce a better quality good or provide a better quality service for the business. Although this can be costly, and also halt productivity as employees may be away from their place of work, it acts to increase motivation as their abilities and self-efficacy increases simultaneously.

Thus, this provides long-term motivation to employees when a business makes a commitment to providing ongoing training options and opportunities for growth and development, as employees know they are provided the opportunity to work to the best of their ability and remain valued and required in the business, improving their levels of motivation into the long term. (10 marks)

VCAA 2020 SA Q4 VCE Business Management examination report

> It's worth taking the time to plan your answer to the 10-mark question in the exam so that you manage your time and thoughts well. It's also important that you don't bring in things that are not mentioned in the question, such as motivational theories. It may not look like there is much to write about here, but when you break the question down, you can see that even the evaluation of two separate motivational strategies requires quite a bit of thought and writing before the application part of the question.

Exam practice: Case study A solutions

> **Note**
> The answers provided for the case study are model answers. They are not necessarily the only correct answers to the questions. Students should check with their teachers to see if their answers would be considered correct.

1 Resignation is when an employee chooses to leave a workplace but is not yet retiring. (1 mark)

2 The staff who are resigning may have annual leave that they have not yet taken. This is paid out when a person resigns. Another entitlement is long service leave. As many of these employees worked at DStore for more than 15 years, they may have also accumulated significant long service leave. If they had not taken all or some of the leave owing to them, it would need to be paid out when they leave the business. (2 marks)

3 It is usual for a business to have the same arrangement for all of its employees; that is, to offer either award wages and conditions, or an enterprise agreement. Sometimes senior managers are excluded and have individual contracts. The advantages of offering award rates is that they are set by the Fair Work Commission and reviewed annually, so no negotiation needs to happen at the workplace. These pay rates tend to be low, hence minimising costs for the business. The difficulty is that low wages are unlikely to attract the best in the field as they can get higher pay rates in other businesses. The advantage of offering an enterprise agreement is that the pay and conditions can be altered to suit the needs of both employees and the employer as long as the employee is better off overall than if they were just on the award rates. While more expensive for DStore, it needs qualified accounting and finance staff who may not apply for jobs that only offer the award rate. (4 marks)

4 Both on-the-job and off-the-job training have the same purpose: to ensure that employees gain the skills that they need in order to do their job. It is the method of delivery of the training that differs. There are more differences than similarities. On-the-job training is usually when one employee trains another in the required skills. It usually happens during the working day in the normal work areas in which the employee operates. Off-the-job training requires the employee to be sent to an external provider to learn the required skills. In the case of DStore, with so many new employees in the one area, it may be beneficial to send all of them to a course to learn about the accounting software so that they won't make errors when they begin. (4 marks)

5 In the first instance, the employee should take their issue to their manager to be resolved. There are usually grievance procedures that are included in the business's policies. The employees' role is to clearly state their concern and allow management the opportunity to resolve the matter at the workplace.

   If the matter is not resolved, it may require mediation. This is where a third party tries to assist the parties to come to a resolution. A participant in this process might be a union representing the interests of the workers in the discussion with the management of the business.

   A third step in the process of dispute resolution is arbitration, where a legally binding decision is made by the Fair Work Commission to resolve the matter of dispute. As a participant, the Fair Work Commission hears from each side and makes a ruling that it considers to be fair in the particular circumstances. (6 marks)

6 A performance appraisal would be an appropriate management strategy for the new employees. This is a formal evaluation of the employees' work over the past year. It would be appropriate because with so many employees starting work in the same section of the business at the same time, a review that looks at their job descriptions and measures their performance in terms of what was required when they were employed may be the best way to determine who is performing well and who requires assistance and support in the future. (3 marks)

Total = 20 marks

Exam practice: Case study B solutions

> **Note**
> The answers provided for the case study are model answers. They are not necessarily the only correct answers to the questions. Students should check with their teachers to see if their answers would be considered to be correct.

1 If employees are managed well, they will be satisfied with their work conditions and are more likely to be productive, to have fewer sick days and to remain loyal to the business. This has a direct link to the business objectives of increased productivity, lower staff absenteeism and lower staff turnover rates. Further, if the employees are managed well they will be appropriately trained and the culture will be positive, leading to good customer service and fewer customer complaints. (2 marks)

2 Maslow believed that people progress through five stages of needs as they mature and develop, moving to the next stage only when the previous one has been satisfied. The stages are physiological needs, safety and security needs, belonging needs, esteem needs and self-actualisation.

   In order to motivate the full-time employees, Eileen would need to determine which levels the workers are at and put in place the things that are necessary to allow workers to satisfy that need. Full-time workers would probably have a desire to feel safe in terms of job security and a reasonable income; therefore, safety and security needs would have to be satisfied. For those with career aspirations, providing the employee with tasks that provide a sense of achievement would satisfy the esteem need. (4 marks)

3 The goal-setting theory's emphasis on the motivation that comes from the achievement of a goal is similar to the Four Drive Theory's drive to acquire, which can relate to recognition of achievement. The differences are that the goal-setting theory is based on the inner sense of achievement that comes from realising specific and challenging goals, while the Four Drive Theory says that there are four different

things that drive employees, and any or all can do this. Casual employees are often not concerned with long-term career goals. The drives to acquire, to bond, to learn and to defend are probably less important to casual employees because they are longer-term strategies.

The Goal Setting Theory of Locke and Latham can be applied to casual employees because the goals can be short term and can be specifically targeted to the skills and talents of each employee at Shako. For this reason, Locke and Latham's Goal Setting Theory would be more effective. (8 marks)

4 a Career advancement could work well to motivate full-time employees because they are more likely to desire stability in their careers and to seek promotion. Many may have mortgages or other commitments that the stability and pay increases related to an advancement in their career could satisfy. The disadvantage of focusing on career advancement to motivate employees is that there is a limit to how many positions can be provided. If employees want to advance, but positions are not available, they may seek employment elsewhere.

b Performance-related pay can be extremely effective to motivate casual employees. In many cases they would only be interested in the fact that there is an income to be derived from their employment. They may not be interested in having a career with the business. The prospect of earning more money can be very attractive and may be enough to motivate the employees to improve their performance. The disadvantage is that such motivational strategies are a cost to the business, which it may not be able to afford or sustain. (3 + 3 = 6 marks)

Total = 20 marks

Chapter 3 Area of Study 3

Exam practice solutions

1 Operations management refers to the task of managing the process that transforms resources into finished goods and/or services.

2 Welding (C) is not an input. It is a process because it helps to transform the input into the finished product (in this case, a car).

3 Computers (D) are not a process. They are an input as they are a resource that is necessary to make the hotel operate. Any work done on the computer (booking reservations, ordering stock, working out rosters, etc.) is considered to be the process.

4 Cooking (B) is not an output. It is a process because it describes what is done to the inputs in order to make the finished product (in this case, fast food).

5 This statement is false. All organisations, especially businesses, create a product. This product can be a good or a service. Whenever a product (output) is made, it is the result of inputs being transformed in some way. This is precisely what operations management is all about, so it does not matter if the firm is a bank or a furniture manufacturer, operations management is equally important.

6 The master production schedule (MPS) should be developed first. The materials requirement plan (MRP) cannot be developed until the MPS is done, because the MPS sets out what and how much of a product must be made within a given time frame. Only then can the operations manager start to think about what materials and how much will be required.

7 'Just in time' materials management only works well if the supply of the necessary stock can be guaranteed. Whenever the supplier has problems with their own production or delivery, this will flow on to the business that has ordered the materials and may cause delays in production or even stop production altogether for a period of time.

8 ISO 9001:2015 is a generic quality management system; this means that it can be applied to any type of business. It is useful for service providers as it is all about the way the product is produced or, in this case, the way the service is provided. ISO 9001:2015 does not require a finished, tangible good as part of its sets of standards.

9 Total Quality Management is a system that is based on the following three concepts:

- a belief in continuous improvement
- the emphasis on teamwork and employee participation to identify and solve problems
- customer satisfaction – both internal and external customers – as the main aim.

10 Efficiency refers to the ability to make the best possible use of resources. Lean manufacturing refers to the establishment of systems that will eliminate waste and inefficiencies of any kind in the process of making a product. Examples of waste include idle time, excess time taken to complete tasks, unused materials, discarded materials, defective products and excessive wait times between production and distribution.

11 Environmental sustainability refers to the process of managing the use of natural resources to ensure that they are not depleted.

12 A restaurant can reduce waste by ordering perishable stock frequently. This way it will hopefully be used before it goes off and becomes waste. A second way that a restaurant can reduce waste is by ensuring that fridges and freezers seal correctly. This way they will not be wasting electricity or the money to pay for their energy bills.

13 One advantage of sourcing inputs from another country is that the costs may be lower. For example, a printing company may source their T-shirts from China because they cost less than Australian-made T-shirts. One disadvantage of sourcing inputs from another country is that jobs may be lost in Australia as businesses do not support the local manufacturers.

14 There are several similarities between robotics and artificial intelligence (AI). Both rely on computer programming and many robots are given AI to enhance the work that they can perform. The differences are that AI does not require robotics and AI can also learn from situations, whereas this is not necessarily a feature of robotics.

15 The main advantage of outsourcing manufacturing is that labour costs are lower in many overseas countries. Blundstone, for example, now outsources the production of all of its boots, except for gumboots, to countries that have lower operating costs. Blundstone does still monitor the quality of its products, even if they have been manufactured less expensively overseas.

16 Sample answer: Shandra's Dairy Ltd could use Just in Time (JIT) as its material management approach. JIT requires managers to order just enough materials for the next production period.

   JIT can increase efficiency as it will ensure that the best use is made of resources – there should be almost no waste, nor should there be shortfalls which stop or slow production in the dairy.

   JIT can also improve effectiveness as it may help the managers of Shandra's Dairy to achieve their objectives such as to make a profit if money is not tied up in excess materials that may not be used. (3 marks)

VCAA 2017 SB Q2 VCE Business Management examination report

17 Sample answer: The key elements of the operations system include inputs, processes and outputs. Inputs are the resources used in the business. For Ocean Skate Hub's operations system this includes labour (their local employees), finances and the location/site of the indoor and outdoor skating parks and the sports products they buy for their sports store.

   Next there is processes. Processes involve the transformation of inputs into outputs (the final product). In relation to Ocean Skate Hub this may include the actual construction of the skating parks and the ordering of sports products for their sports shop. In relation to their café, that could involve the making of coffee for their customers.

   The outputs is the last element and involves the final product that is served to the customers. This for Ocean Skate would be quality services from the café, sports products from the store and quality experiences at the skating parks. (6 marks)

VCAA 2018 SB Q2 VCE Business Management examination report

While it is easy to apply the key elements of operations (inputs, processes and outputs) to a manufacturing firm, it becomes more difficult when the business is a service provider like Ocean Hub in this case study.

18 Sample answer: The first stage of operations relate to inputs; these are the resources used to create an end output. For a manufacturing business like ChocYum Pty Ltd inputs are vital including cocoa and sugar but most importantly staff to run and operate the machines. Similarly to a service such as a haircut human resources are an essential part of operations that are required to create the end output.

However, they differ in the processes stage which relates to transforming inputs to outputs as often a manufacturing business is able to automate production using machines though a service business like haircuts can't do this.

Finally, the other key difference is in outputs which relates to the end product, a manufacturing business like ChocYum Pty Ltd create a tangible output that can be stored. Unlike a service business like a haircut who can't store a haircut and it is intangible. (4 marks)

VCAA 2019 SA Q1b VCE Business Management examination report

It is important to note here that while ChocYum is mentioned in the question, it just says 'such as', so it is not essential to refer to it in the response. If, however, this question was in Section B of the exam, then reference to the case study would be essential. As always, 'compare' questions require students to describe both similarities and differences.

19 Sample answer: Chef@Home could introduce lean management, which is an ongoing management philosophy, whereby they seek to reduce wastage in each area of the business while still providing quality and value to customers. They can adopt the 'pull focused' principle whereby they only prepare and package the required amount of meals as demanded by customers, perhaps after they order it online. This will minimise wastage in terms of overproduction of pre-made meals that will not be sold and thus have to be discarded. They can also minimise waste in regards to time through adopting the 'flow' principle, and minimising any wait times in their preparation and packaging of meals. Reducing starts and stops and bottle necks will minimise time that may otherwise be wasted improving the efficiency of operations. (3 marks)

VCAA 2020 SA Q5a VCE Business Management examination report

The Study Design refers to the reduction of waste (reduce, reuse, recycle) as a specific strategy; however, it is also the purpose of lean production and one of the main aims of materials management. Therefore, it is vital that you read any questions relating to waste very carefully to see if the examiners are looking for a specific strategy response. The sample answer here refers to lean production.

20 Sample answer: Forecasting is a materials management strategy that uses data from the past and present and analysis of trends in attempts to determine future events. An advantage of forecasting is that it allows Chef@Home to identify what needs to be produced, in what quantities, how and when. This will result in 'all inputs from local suppliers' actually being used and not wasted, thus assisting to improve efficiency of operations as Chef@Home is able to better utilise their resources.

Moreover, Chef@Home using forecasting to order inputs from local suppliers in advance avoids the risk of having to outsource to other suppliers as they do not have enough inputs currently to supply boxes.

As a result of this, Chef@Home will be improving the effectiveness of its operations as it is able to order inputs in advance to ensure all inputs are from local suppliers, thus improving the business objectives of all locally sourced inputs. However, a disadvantage of forecasting is that it will represent a cost to Chef@Home if the wrong quantities are calculated as it will lead to overproduction or underproduction. Overall, forecasting would be good to improve operations as it ensures that all local sourced inputs will be used. (4 marks)

VCAA 2020 SA Q5b VCE Business Management examination report

As with all of the operations management strategies, you will need to be able to explain, or in this case analyse, how the strategy can increase BOTH efficiency and effectiveness. This question also specifically requires you to apply your response to the Chef@Home situation as described in the 2020 Exam.

Exam practice: Case study solutions

1 Inputs are the resources used to make a good or provide a service. Thunder Sportswear requires fabric to make the football jumpers and other clothing. Another input is design software programs for the creation of the patterns of the range of products manufactured by Thunder Sportswear. (3 marks)

2 Processes are the actions performed on inputs to create the final products. Cutting the fabric is one process necessary to make the football jumpers. Sewing the garment pieces together to create the jumpers and other clothing is a second process. (3 marks)

3 If the operations are managed effectively and efficiently, there will be minimal waste and the quality of the good or service will be high. More customers are likely to purchase the products and place repeat orders, which will make the achievement of the business objectives of increased profit, number of sales and market share more likely to occur. (2 marks)

4 Goods are products that are tangible, can be stored for later use and the consumption can occur separately from the purchase. Books are examples of goods.

 Services, on the other hand, are products that are intangible, they cannot be stored and the consumption usually occurs with the purchase, meaning that the consumer is involved directly. An example of a service is a haircut. (2 marks)

5 Just in Time (JIT) would be an appropriate materials strategy in this situation. JIT is a materials strategy that is implemented as part of the supply chain whereby just enough materials are kept on hand to get the workplace through the next production period. Thunder Sportswear had ordered large amounts of fabric, which are now found to be faulty. If JIT was implemented, there would be minimal unusable stock tying up money and space in the factory. (1 + 2 + 2 = 5 marks)

6 The level of waste would be an appropriate key performance indicator. The waste in this case would be unused fabric, as it has been found to be faulty. If the business uses Just in Time as a strategy when ordering stock, the result should be less waste, even if faults are detected because less stock would be kept on hand. (2 marks)

7 Quality control would be effective because Jacqui could test all fabrics as they arrive at Thunder Sportswear to determine if they are faulty. Quality control requires a series of checks as to whether products or services meet internal standards. A difficulty with quality control is that it may be too late if the fabric has already arrived and production lines could be held up if the fabric fails the checks. Quality assurance, on the other hand, could prove to be effective because it is a quality method that involves measuring the quality of a product or process against a standard (domestic or international). External audits can result in gaining quality assurance certification. While the quality problems at Thunder Sportswear may lie with the fabric supplier, the company could insist that all suppliers meet an external standard such as ISO 9001 to ensure that it does not receive faulty products in the future. In this situation, it could be simpler to just perform quality checks on future fabric supplies when they arrive, before manufacturing the clothing begins. (6 marks)

8 Efficiency relates to making the best use of resources. The levels of waste have increased by 10% at Thunder Sportswear so technology that could reduce the levels of waste would also increase efficiency. Pattern-making software would be appropriate because it would allow the designers to work out the most effective way to cut the pattern pieces to maximise the use of the fabric, resulting in less offcuts. The result would be an increase in efficiency. (4 marks)

9 Lean production refers to the establishment of systems that will eliminate waste and inefficiencies of any kind in the process of making a good or providing a service. The levels of waste have increased at Thunder Sportswear, and waste equals lost money. By establishing lean principles, Jacqui can ensure that there is no wasted fabric, but also minimise other types of waste such as idle time and defective products. She might find that there are excessive wait times between production and delivery that are causing the customer complaints, and lean principles such as takt and zero defects should minimise the likelihood of this happening. (4 marks)

10 The main advantage of purchasing fabric from an overseas supplier is that it is likely to be less expensive than the locally made product because of the cheaper labour costs in other countries. The disadvantages are that Thunder Sportswear could no longer claim to have an entirely 'Australian-made' product, and there would be a time delay in receiving the product. Even though they have experienced difficulties with the quality of the fabric lately, the turnaround to get replacement stock would be fast because the suppliers are based in Victoria. Customers may appreciate the fact that the products are entirely Australian made; therefore, purchasing fabric from an overseas supplier may not be entirely advantageous to Thunder Sportswear. (6 marks)

11 Corporate social responsibility is where businesses take responsibility, through the use of ethical practices, for any actions that affect the wider community. Thunder Sportswear could consider the effect on the environment of the processes that are involved in the manufacture of the sports clothing. Where possible, fabric offcuts could be recycled or donated to charities if they would be of any use. This will minimise the amount of waste that ends up in landfill. (3 marks)

Total = 40 marks

UNIT 4: TRANSFORMING A BUSINESS

Chapter 4 Area of Study 1

Exam practice solutions

1 Businesses monitor their performance so that they know if they are achieving their objectives. If their performance is slipping, it can indicate that they might need to plan a change to improve their success.

2 A large building construction company would need to carefully monitor the number of workplace accidents. Dangerous equipment would be used and there may be scaffolding to climb for multistorey buildings. If the number of workplace accidents increases, then they may need to review their occupational health and safety policies and procedures.

3 Market share would be appropriate as a key performance indicator (KPI) to evaluate the success of a supermarket. The supermarket industry is highly competitive. Customers will vote with their dollars as they shop at their preferred supermarket. If one supermarket can entice customers to come to them and leave their competitor, hence increasing their market share, then they will know that they are doing the right things.

4 Yes, a business can increase sales while reducing its net profit. This is because profit is the result of revenue minus expenses. Increased revenue will only lead to increased profit if the costs remain the same or decrease. If the costs go up at an amount that is greater than the increased revenue from sales, then the profit will actually decrease.

5 Staff absenteeism and staff turnover are similar in that they are both KPIs that relate to employees. In both cases employers would like the rates to be low, because if they are high, it can reflect a problem in the business.

They are different, however, because staff absenteeism measures the rate at which staff are taking days off work, while staff turnover measures the rate at which staff leave and are replaced in a business.

6 Force Field Analysis is a theory developed by Kurt Lewin that states that driving forces must push through restraining forces if change is to occur. Once the forces have been ranked and weighted, it may require a strategy to reduce the restraining forces or strengthen the driving forces so that the change can occur.

7 Employees could be the driving force behind change if they can see work practices that are unsafe. They may push the managers of the business to implement new occupational health and safety policies and procedures. Employees could also be the driving force behind the implementation of work–life balance policies. For example, employees may request that the business allow employees to work from home even if there is no health advice suggesting this. After the COVID-19 lockdown experience, the employees may have found that the time gained from no travel to the workplace enhances their lives.

8 Most businesses want to pursue profit. This drives businesses to innovate and seek new markets. The drive to reduce costs, however, may be to minimise wasted capital. By reducing costs, the business may increase its net profit, but this may just be a side benefit of the change rather than the primary objective.

9 Restraining forces are factors that repress or block pressures for change.

10 Employees may resist change because they fear for their job security. If the change could result in people being made redundant, then this could create resistance from the employees.

Employees may also resist change because they disagree with it. If they are experienced workers, they may feel that the change is not in the best interests of the business and therefore they resist it.

11 Competitive advantage is the state where one business is in a more favourable state than its rivals due to lower costs or differentiation.

12 The five competitive forces are:
- the entry of new competitors
- the threat of substitutes
- the bargaining power of buyers
- the bargaining power of suppliers
- the rivalry among existing competitors.

13 One advantage of prioritising cost leadership is that it will attract customers who base their purchasing decisions on the prices of goods and services. This can give a business a competitive advantage.

One disadvantage of prioritising cost leadership is that compromises may have to be made in terms of quality to keep prices down. This may turn away some customers who are willing to pay higher prices to ensure that the goods are high quality.

14 Apple iPhones are seen as different from other smartphones. Because of this, some customers are willing to pay higher prices for them.

Supermarkets differentiate their products from their competitors. They focus on 'fresh food' or the use of celebrity chefs to create a point of difference. By doing this, they attract customers who don't mind paying more for products than they would if they shopped at a discount supermarket.

15 This statement is false. The focus strategy is where managers target a narrow segment of the market. They offer a niche product to a very particular group of potential customers.

16 Sample answer: One driving force could be the managers of Shandra's Dairy. The managers could see the financial benefits of operating globally and may push to make the change happen. It would be unlikely to proceed without the managers driving this change, as they will be responsible for most of the research and implementation work to make this happen.

One restraining force would be financial considerations. Operating globally requires a large financial outlay, especially as the establishment stage. A cost/benefit analysis would be essential to see if Shandra's Dairy could actually afford such a move, or whether the cost would be prohibitive. (4 marks)

VCAA 2017 SB Q6 VCE Business Management examination report

17
- Begin by explaining why leadership is important when managing change. Link this to making it easier to overcome resistance to change.
- Briefly outline the business that you are using as your example and describe the change they were undertaking.
- Explain how effective leadership helped the business to manage the change or explain how the change failed or was not fully successful because there was a lack of leadership during the change process. Both of these approaches will show how important leadership is during a period of change. (6 marks)

VCAA 2018 SA Q2 VCE Business Management examination report

This question requires you to refer to a real, contemporary (from the past 4 years) business case study. You cannot use a fictional case study, so it is important that you have a number of these ready for each Area of Study. Don't forget that if you have a part-time job, or if you know some businesses well, you may be able to use them for examples even if you didn't study them at school.

18 Sample answer: Dennis used the strategy of differentiation to respond to the issues of declining sales and changing customer tastes. Differentiation involves creating a point of uniqueness or distinctiveness in business operation from other competitors in the market. Dennis' burger chain has decided to become more environmentally and economically sustainable than rivals in the burger industry by sourcing ethical and high-quality local ingredients. This creates demand for Dennis' burgers as they are different to others on the market giving Dennis freedom to charge a premium price for his burgers as customers become loyal to his business. Attitudes among society are shifting towards sustainability focus and by taking advantage of this Dennis's addressing the shift in the business environment. This may lead to an increase in the number of sales at his restaurant due to his unique ingredients and sustainable approach. (4 marks)

VCAA 2019 SA Q5b VCE Business Management examination report

A knowledge of both of Porter's strategies is required here, but it is the analysis that gives this question a degree of difficulty. Going back to the prompt material before beginning the answer would be beneficial in this case.

19 Sample answer: Change can be undertaken as a proactive or reactive approach. Being proactive means that the managers are making changes to improve the business in anticipation of what might be ahead. They may be trend-setting in terms of product development or improved processes. Being proactive can keep a business ahead of its competitors and ensure that valuable employees will want to stay.

A reactive approach, however, may be necessary if something has gone wrong or was unforeseen. There may be an internal problem to fix or the business may find that competitors have the edge and they need to catch up. (4 marks)

VCAA 2019 SA Q2 VCE Business Management examination report

Simple definitions of these terms will not be enough to be awarded the full four marks. It requires examples to show how change can be managed as well.

20 Sample answer: KPI 1: The KPI of number of customer complaints could be used by Manitta Mining to assess business performance. If the business can maintain low levels of customer complaints, it indicates to management that they are responding to the needs of customers through the provision of high-quality mining services. Therefore, it demonstrates that the organisation is performing to a high standard, as fewer customers complaining indicates that Manitta Mining is meeting the expectations of their customers and clients. If complaints were to increase, it may indicate to the CEO an issue with quality or an increased need for staff training.

KPI 2: Another KPI that could be used is percentage of market share, which indicates the percentage of the market that Manitta Mining has control of within the mining sector. A high percentage of market share indicates that consumers prefer Manitta Mining over competitors, suggesting they have high levels of quality and thus satisfied customers. It also indicates that Manitta is producing higher levels of profit than their competitors. Both of these factors indicate to the CEO and upper management that Manitta is performing at an extremely high level. (6 marks)

VCAA 2020 SB Q4 VCE Business Management examination report

It is important to read this question carefully, because it excludes the following KPIs that were mentioned in the speech:

- level of staff turnover
- number of workplace accidents
- rate of productivity growth
- number of sales
- rates of staff absenteeism.

That only leaves the following KPIs from the list in the Study Design:

- net profit figures
- percentage of market share
- level of waste
- number of customer complaints.

You can, however, use other KPIs that are not mentioned in the Study Design if they are relevant to this case study.

Exam practice: Case study A solutions

> **Note**
> The answers provided for the case study are model answers. They are not necessarily the only correct answers to the questions. Students should check with their teachers to see if their answers would be considered correct.

1 a Restraining forces are factors that repress or block pressures for change.

b Staff turnover is measured by the rate at which staff leave and are replaced in a business.

c Profit is the money left over when expenses are deducted from revenue. (1 + 1 + 1 = 3 marks)

2 The Force Field Analysis is a theory developed by Lewin that states that driving forces must push through restraining forces if change is to occur. A business cannot sustain the increased levels of staff turnover and workplace accidents; therefore, a change must take place. Anouk must decide what that change will be, then work to identify and push through any resistance to make the change successful. Employees would probably be happy to see her tackling the levels of staff turnover and workplace accidents, but if the proposed changes increase prices or affect the way that dogs are treated or controlled, there could be resistance from customers that needs to be overcome. It is up to Anouk to rank and weight the forces to see if there is sufficient strength in the driving forces to make the change occur. (6 marks)

3 Occupational health and safety legislation could be a driving force for change. The number of workplace accidents mainly as a result of dog bites have increased, so WorkSafe may be involved and Pretty Pooches may have no choice but to change. If employees are having to take leave as a result of WorkCover claims, it becomes a very expensive process for the business. On the other hand, if Pretty Pooches abides by the relevant legislation, then it may not push for any changes to occur.

The pursuit of profit can also be a driving force for change. While profits are increasing, Anouk may feel comfortable, but this must be measured against the negative KPIs such as the staff turnover rate. The cost of constantly replacing staff can be very high. If staff are not happy and are leaving, the business's reputation as an employer may suffer and it may not be able to attract skilled employees. This would ultimately affect the profit levels of the business. On the other hand, it may be the case that Anouk is quite happy with small increases in profit and does not feel that the pressure to make more money drives her to make any changes at all. (8 marks)

4 Sometimes a business owner or manager would like to make changes but simply cannot afford to. This could be the case where there is better, more efficient machinery that could speed up the production process, but the cost is simply too high for the business to take on. (2 marks)

5 Lower cost options can be beneficial because they can increase market share as customers seek the best price for dog grooming services. Pretty Pooches increased its profit by 20% over the past year, so it could possibly reduce costs and still remain profitable.

Differentiation refers to having a unique point of difference from competitors. Pretty Pooches may decide to focus on grooming show dogs or specialise in fancy clipping of dogs' coats. Alternatively, Anouk could decide to focus on the accessories – perhaps an exclusive range of products that cannot be sourced easily in Australia.

While both options would probably be suitable for Anouk's business, differentiating the product may be the best option. In this way Anouk would not have to raise her prices or lower her costs. She may even be able to increase her prices if the unique products prove to be popular, giving her the money to address the staff turnover rate and workplace accident issues properly. (6 marks)

Total = 25 marks

Exam practice: Case study B solutions

> **Note**
> The answers provided for the case study are model answers. They are not necessarily the only correct answers to the questions. Students should check with their teachers to see if their answers would be considered correct.

1 Business change refers to the process that alters the existing state of aspects of a business and creates a new form of them. (1 mark)

2 Kurt Lewin developed the Force Field Analysis theory, which looked at the factors that were helpful in achieving a goal (driving forces) against those that hinder or prevent the achievement of the goal (restraining forces). In order for change to occur, the equilibrium or balance between the two forces must be broken, with the driving forces winning through. For example, if a manager wanted to install new technology throughout the business, but employees resisted, it would be unlikely to happen unless the forces pushing the change were strong enough to break through the employees' resistance. Their ability to do this depends on the weight of each force. (4 marks)

3 One driving force could be to reduce costs. Profit levels are falling at Eduk8ed, so if the costs of production are proving to be too expensive, Ian Indigo might feel that this needs to be addressed.

  Societal attitudes could be another driving force. A social enterprise responds to needs in the community that it aims to help. While management is not concerned about market share per se, the limited increase in sales and lower profit would affect the business's ability to assist needy children and this could drive it to implement changes in response. (4 marks)

4 A similarity between differentiation and lower costs is that they are both possible options that business owners and/or managers may face when confronted with data to which they need to respond. They are both fundamental options for changing a business.

  The differences, however, are greater than the point of similarity. Differentiation refers to creating a unique point of difference from a business's competitors. Lower cost is a deliberate strategy of reducing production costs to become a cost leader. This can be done in many ways, such as seeking lower cost materials or reducing labour costs. The choice made may depend on the target customer of the business and its ability to pay high prices for products. (4 marks)

5 Even if profit levels remain high (and they are actually falling in this case study), the levels of waste would still be of concern. Waste is the result of inefficiencies. Wasted materials are an unnecessary expense of the business. Given that Eduk8ed is a social enterprise, a greater number of school children could be helped if the waste levels were lower. There is also the environmental issue. Waste must be disposed of. If wasted materials end up in landfill, that is environmentally undesirable and probably contradicts the corporate social responsibility policies of Eduk8ed. (4 marks)

6 Employees may resist a strategy of lower costs if the impact is felt on their wages. This could slow the process of change as managers negotiate with the employees. If unions become involved, the matter could be prolonged.

  Organisational inertia is a state that can develop within a business that is not open and receptive to change. As Eduk8ed has existed for more than 10 years, a culture may have developed where everyone is quite comfortable with the way that things are currently done. Employees may not see the need for any change and could therefore not be open to the process. The culture may need to change to remove the organisational inertia and allow the lower costs strategy to proceed. (6 marks)

7 Profit is the result of revenue minus expenses. If the revenue received from sales increases, it will not be reflected in the profits unless the business costs remain the same or fall. If the business's expenses have increased significantly, the net profit will decrease. (2 marks)

Total = 25 marks

Chapter 5 Area of Study 2

Exam practice solutions

1 Effective leadership will generate trust among employees, leading to less resistance to change. This assists in creating a smooth change process.

2 Changing a management style from autocratic to participative may lead to employees taking ownership of business decisions. This could lead to a lower staff turnover rate as well as a lower staff absenteeism rate because the employees will enjoy being at their workplace.

3 A coffee shop could cut its costs to increase its profits. This could be done by finding lower cost suppliers of essential products such as coffee and sugar.

   A second way that a coffee shop could increase its profits is by implementing lean principles into its production. This will ensure that there is no waste; therefore, no money is lost in this area, leading to an increase in net profit.

4 A business could access new opportunities within Australia by differentiating its product. This will attract new customers. The business could also seek financial help from government business authorities to assist it to branch out into new areas and access new opportunities.

5 Austrade provides businesses with information and advice about exporting and doing business in other countries.

6 Learning Organisations are those where employees are encouraged to work in teams with a shared vision to continually learn.

7 Systems thinking integrates the other four disciplines, allowing them to make sense as a cohesive management practice.

8 There are three steps in Lewin's change model: unfreeze, change and refreeze. Unfreeze means removing inertia and preparing stakeholders for the change. In the change stage, new processes or practices may be introduced to the business. The refreeze step is where a new stability and culture is established.

9 The first stage of Lewin's theory relates to his Force Field Analysis theory. It is during the 'unfreeze' stage that the driving forces need to push through the restraining forces to allow the change to occur.

10 After completion of the process of change, managers and owners need to continue to monitor their business's performance through KPIs. This is because circumstances in any of the three environments may have changed, leading to new driving forces applying pressure for further changes to be made.

11 Low-risk strategies are methods of introducing change that are likely to be well accepted with little resistance.

12 Managers need to communicate the changes clearly, making sure that all stakeholders are aware of the process that will be undertaken and the benefits that should result. When the details of changes are fully explained, employees may find that it's not as bad as they feared and may be happy to support the changes. A second way to encourage employee support for a change is to involve them. If employees are empowered to make decisions and offer suggestions about the change process, then they are less likely to resist it.

13 Manipulation of information in order to push through a change can create distrust, lower morale and damage the corporate culture. It can also create further problems as workers are less likely to conform to the changes if they feel that they have been misled.

14 The long-term effects of high-risk strategies to implement change are likely to cause further problems for the business. If the change process was not grounded in trust and respect, then there is little chance that the employees will be supportive of all aspects of the change.

15 Managers need to evaluate the effectiveness of the business transformation so that they can see if the time and effort that went into the process was worth it. A cost–benefit analysis could clarify this situation. If it has not been successful, then perhaps the managers need to formulate a different plan.

16 Sample answer: The Three-step Change Model provides a scaffold which a business can follow to implement successful changes. The first step, unfreeze, is about opening up the business to a state where it has the momentum to undergo the change. This involves communicating a vision for the change to stakeholders and creating a sense of urgency for the change. Shandra's Dairy Ltd could unfreeze by first communicating a vison of the snack foods that they are hoping to implement and highlighting the benefits of the expansion to key stakeholders to get them on board with the change.

The next step, change, is about moving towards the desired state of the business by transforming and involves providing ongoing support and dedicating the necessary resources towards the change. Shandra's Dairy Ltd could empower employees to get them working towards developing the new snack foods and allocate the necessary resources towards expanding the product range in order to provide a smooth transition.

The final stage, refreeze, is about reinforcing the change into the business so it will not revert to old ways. This involves anchoring the changes into the culture and making necessary adjustments. Shandra's Dairy Ltd should provide ongoing training to staff who have taken on new roles in the snack food production and allow for new suggestions and product innovations so that the business will continue its commitment to the expanded product range and snack foods. (6 marks)

VCAA 2017 SB Q4 VCE Business Management examination report

For six marks, you need to do more than just list the three steps. You need to show an understanding of what each step means within the context of the case study that was provided.

17 Sample answer: Support is a low-risk strategy because it is unlikely to have negative consequences. It can come in a variety of forms such as encouragement or offering training. If Dennis offers support to his executive chef in the form of further training, it would show him that he is valued and included as the change occurs. This should result in the chef being supportive of the change which makes it easier for Dennis to implement it. (3 marks)

VCAA 2019 SA Q5c VCE Business Management examination report

Careful reading of the question is important here, as it is asking specifically about the strategy of 'support', not any of the other low-risk strategies.

18 Sample answer: Lewin's Three-step Change Model can be implemented to help facilitate effective change.

The first step is to unfreeze the business. Dennis can do this to prepare his business for change and includes identifying what must change, the pricing strategy, then Dennis can create an urgency for change by demonstrating a need for the new prices to his employees, before finally challenging the status quo at Dennis's burgers that may resist the new pricing strategy.

With the business unfrozen and prepared for change Dennis can now go about moving towards the new desired state by implementing the new pricing strategy. It is important that Dennis uses support and clear communication to his employees during this stage to enable its successful implementation. Supporting employees throughout this process, especially those that are struggling with the new pricing strategy, is important so that the transition at Dennis's business is as smooth as possible. (4 marks)

VCAA 2019 SA Q5d VCE Business Management examination report

It's the application part of this question that makes it a little more difficult. The trick is to carefully select the two steps that you think you can best apply to the scenario that you have been given.

19 Sample answer: Many businesses had to go through reactive change due to the global pandemic of COVID-19. Particularly supermarket businesses responsible for supplying the society with essential products for survival. As an effective leader, Brad Banducci, CEO of Woolworths, has led his business in an efficient way to respond to the change.

Driving forces are those that support and encourage change and thus, aids in accomplishing business objectives and ensures the success of the change. Societal attitudes are a major driving force. These relate to the changing attitudes and beliefs of the wider community. COVID-19 sent many customers/society into a panic state of purchasing an excessive amount of essentials for the survival of lockdown. This led to Brad's response to change the way Woolworths runs, in order to accurately respond to the changed societal attitudes towards purchasing essentials.

Brad needed to quickly respond to this by introducing a limit as to how much items an individual could purchase (as he needed to ensure there is always enough stock considering the panic buying). Not only this, but also open up Woolworths stores an hour early, dedicated to only the elderly as societal attitudes also changed towards them as they were considered most vulnerable and thus, had more priorities to gain essential items over those of a younger age. Therefore, Brad used societal attitudes as a way that drove his business to change, which he handled adequately and had been successful and efficient during the pandemic. (6 marks)

VCAA 2020 SA Q6 VCE Business Management examination report

> The examination report makes the following comment for this question.
> Three basic components were needed for this response:
> - explanation of a change that had occurred in a business within the past 4 years
> - explanation of what the societal attitude was that drove the specific change
> - explanation of how that societal attitude had driven the business to make the change.

20 Sample answer: Restraining force 1: Legislation are the laws set by the government which all businesses must follow, otherwise there will be fines or possible imprisonment. This is a restraining force as the Australian Government may place a limit on the amount of brown coal to be mined each year. This could limit Manitta Mining from growing their business. Preventing change from occurring, hindering Manitta Mining's business activity. Preventing successful change of expansion.

Restraining force 2: Financial considerations will be restraining cost as the business may have to pay large amounts to update mining machinery and technology, such as trucks. Although this may be too expensive for Manitta Mining, as it could lead to negative net profit figures, which would lead to a reduction in the market share price, which could unsettle the shareholders. This will limit and inhibit the benefits of updating technology to have a successful change. (4 marks)

VCAA 2020 SB Q6 VCE Business Management examination report

> Go back to the case study to decide which two restraining forces from the list would be easiest for you to address and link to the case study. You cannot write about other restraining forces for this question.

Exam practice: Case study solutions

> **Note**
> The answers provided for the case study are model answers. They are not necessarily the only correct answers to the questions. Students should check with their teachers to see if their answers would be considered correct.

1 Leadership is very important during a period of change. If strong leadership qualities are shown, more trust will be gained from employees, leading to less resistance to change. This can allow the change process to occur more quickly and with a greater chance of success. (2 marks)

2 Net profit has increased by 2%. This is not a huge increase, so if Coop's Mobile Homes (CMH) wanted to increase its profits, it could try to reduce its costs. This could be done by sourcing less expensive inputs, such as the appliances that are built into the mobile homes.

The level of staff turnover is unchanged. This indicates that employees are satisfied with CMH and do not feel the need to seek employment elsewhere. But if this KPI is looked at in conjunction with the 30% increase in staff absenteeism, it could reflect a deeper problem. Managers would need to look at whether the employees are taking advantage of lenient conditions. Or it could be the case that there are factors at work that are making people take time off. A strategy would be to initially investigate why people are taking so many days off. If they are injuring themselves at work, then perhaps they need training in how to better operate machinery.

The level of waste has increased by 15%. A strategy to combat this would be to introduce lean principles of production. This would detect the types of waste that are excessive, then provide solutions for ways to minimise it. At CMH the waste may be that there is too much idle time where workers have little to do, or perhaps the materials used to construct the retro vans are not used well. Either way, lean production should provide solutions to the problems. (12 marks)

3 Blair is looking at exporting to the United States and Canada. Accessing the services provided by Austrade could be a very effective strategy for Blair. Austrade provides general information about exporting and doing business in international markets, free of charge to Australian companies. This information could pave the way for Blair to pursue this change of business direction. (2 marks)

4 Learning Organisations are those in which employees are encouraged to work in teams with a shared vision to continually learn. There are five disciplines that must be in place for a Learning Organisation to occur.

- Personal mastery: This is increasing proficiency and expertise in work and becoming committed to lifelong learning.
- Mental models: These are deeply held assumptions, generalisations or even pictures or images that must reflect the business's desired positions to be effective.
- Building a shared vision: People's individual visions need to be changed to that of a shared vision for the whole organisation.
- Team learning: This places emphasis on the team as more is likely to be achieved if there is team learning.
- Systems thinking: This is how managers can see the entire organisation, rather than small segments. (4 marks)

5 Threatening workers' job security in order to implement change might be effective in the short term, but may have negative consequences in the long term. This is a high-risk strategy because if the employees are genuinely unwell, threatening them with consequences, such as no pay for absences or losing their jobs, could backfire on the business.

Support is a low-risk strategy that can be applied in the form of training, encouragement or even financial support. Managers also need to be aware of the fears or concerns that employees and other stakeholders may have regarding the change, and then offer support. Given that Blair aims to tackle the levels of staff absenteeism, support might be effective, but there are costs associated in terms of time and finance. If Blair wants to retain his low staff turnover rate, he would be better off using support as a low-risk strategy to deal with the issue of high absenteeism. (6 marks)

6 The first step in Lewin's change model is to unfreeze the current situation. This involves preparing stakeholders for the change. Stakeholders in this case could be the CMH sales team, who may need to seek overseas customers and the employees who need to be made aware of the plans.

The second step in Lewin's model is to change. This is where new manufacturing processes may be introduced to CMH and sales are sought in the United States and Canada. Support and/or training may need to be provided to employees who may need to learn new ways of building vans to conform to other countries' standards.

The final step of Lewin's change model is to refreeze the business to establish a new stability and culture – in this case as an exporter of caravans. This should now become the usual way of doing things at Coop's Mobile Homes. (1 mark for identifying each step, 1 mark for explaining it and 1 mark for applying it × 3 steps = 9 marks)

7 Stakeholders are those who have an interest in a business or those who may be affected by the business's decisions. CMH sales staff may find that they now need to travel overseas to try to drum up sales of the vans in Canada and the United States.

Manufacturing employees could require training because the exported caravans may require different electrical sockets or they may need to conform to international safety standards that could be different from those in Australia.

Manufacturers of caravans based in the United States and Canada will be affected by CMH's decision. They will be faced with a new rival that will be vying for market share. The novelty of vans from Australia could prove to be a serious threat to their sales. (6 marks)

8 Blair needs to keep corporate social responsibility and community expectations regarding ethical behaviour in mind while changing to become an exporter of caravans. For example, if the vans destined to be shipped overseas require different electrical systems, Blair would need to make sure that the products are sourced from companies that treat their own employees ethically. While it could be cheaper to source products from companies that do not pay their own employees a fair wage, it would be unethical to do so. (4 marks)

9 Blair decided to export caravans because his profit levels were only increasing by 2% over the past year. The pursuit of the export market exposes the business to many more potential customers than those in Australia, hopefully translating into increased sales and profits. If, after a year of trying to break into overseas markets, the profits remain steady or even fall, then Blair would need to decide if the change was worthwhile and whether he would be better off remaining as a domestic supplier. It could be the case that initial set-up costs were high, so it may take a couple of years to return to profitability. Only by evaluating the data can Blair determine if the change has been effective in achieving the business's objectives. (5 marks)

Total = 50 marks